A Pathway to an Ending

Fred Madryga

Glass House Books
Brisbane

Glass House Books
an imprint of IP (Interactive Publications Pty Ltd)
Treetop Studio • 9 Kuhler Court
Carindale, Queensland, Australia 4152
sales@ipoz.biz
http://ipoz.biz/

Printed in 12 pt Adobe Caslon Pro on 14 pt Avenir Book.

ISBN: 9780978281755 (PB); 978 (eBk)

Glass House Books

A Pathway to an Ending

One might think that a person would be sure of their own name. I always thought mine was Frederick. Then one day my 90-year-old Mum said; "Fred you don't spell your name like that." She was right too. It is Fredrick, no 'e,' according to my birth certificate. In addition to correcting how I spelled my name, Mum, who loved me, told me on separate occasions not to worry so much and not to toot my own horn. It wasn't all that hard to avoid tooting. But being raised around the Fraser River canyon and in the east end of Vancouver BC, things to worry about were easy to find.

I was able to achieve a doctorate in Psychology in my mid-30s. Guess which first name is on the sheepskin? The time it took to achieve such a goal was due to time-outs while working at many jobs along the way. From the age of 15 I included working in construction, logging, roofing, cladding and sheet metal work. I even had an early hiatus working at a club for the well-to-do. Later, I taught at a college and then ran my own private psychology practice.

I played sports such as football and lacrosse in my late teens and early twenties and then badminton and judo back at university. Hunting, fishing and target shooting continued until my middle seventies. I found Tai Chi in my fifties and periodically go back to it.

My father told me there would always be greater and lesser people in my life, and there were. He said to read between the lines and to look ahead, and I tried and still do. He added that I should believe nothing I hear and only half of what I see. And, he gave me a prayer to recite when asking God to help me keep my mouth shut: "Oh lord help me keep my trap shut until I know what I am talking about."

You know what? In the end, I have usually been good enough. I have also had love in my life. My job now is to feel the grief of watching, supporting, and loving my partner of 45 years as she becomes ill and begins to struggle. "One fight more..."

Glass House Books
Brisbane

DEDICATION

Patricia Jarvis, a master teacher, who showed me what a great teacher is while inspiring so many young students over the years.

Patricia Ross, who provided support through the tough early years while working and creating two children along the way.

Michael and Daniel, our two sons.

CONTENTS

ACKNOWLEDGMENTS

Light from the setting sun coming through the windows above me in the library that evening many years ago was painting everything with a tinge of orange. Sitting there in the silence with no one else around, I felt a strong feeling of connection beginning to develop in me. The author of the article I was reading (Johann Prus) lived and did his work in the late 1800s. My time was nearing the end of the 20th century. His study of motor seizures and measurement of after discharges in the brain before the development of EEG recorders amazed me. I admired what he had done. I even felt we would understand each other if only we could talk. It was a special feeling and very strong. Others have felt such a connection. I especially remember Raphael Lorente de No, who wrote that Santiago Ramon y Cajal had been before him after using the electron microscope to study Cajal's work in the cerebellum. De No had felt that connection across the years, and now I had felt it, too. Reading what was said in the articles made me feel part of something larger than myself. Over time, the feeling became one of gratitude for those who had preceded me.

I want to make the first acknowledgment to those who have gone before us. Humble or famous, they struggled mightily and intelligently while managing to deliver a kinder and more optimistic time than the one they lived in. I am not sure that my generation has done so well, but my gratitude for those who have gone before me remains. Others are always part of our work, and the merit found there. It is also true that any mistakes we make are not theirs but ours alone.

The first individual I wish to thank is Terry McGarvey. He was the friend who drew the picture in the frontispiece. It should have read 'psychology' instead of 'sociology,' but he would laugh about that. Despite diverging pathways, Terry, I carried your friendship with me. Mike and Susan Oster are also gone. Thank you for your company, your friendship and your interest in my writing. An editor at Friesen

Press called my directing comments to the reader 'breaking the fourth wall.' Would you remember discussing this very thing with me? How I wish you were here so you could see where the writing went. With Patricia Ross, the three of you represent a life lesson. One shouldn't leave thanking people for so long that it is posthumous. If you do, you will regret it, as I do.

Those who helped, and are still living, include Richard and Cherry Whitaker. Still friends after all these years. Thank you for your comments and support. Stephen Burles and Sibell Hackney, thank you as well, especially for your opinions. You have been beautiful bell-weathers for truth, clarity and emotional validity. Now, you have done an author introduction and made a wonderful book cover. Dr. David Reiter, it wasn't just your reaction to my first humble effort that helped make these stories appear; one of your poems helped, too. And now you and Interactive Publications Pty Ltd are editing and facilitating the publication of the work. Thank you, David. Jamie Charmin, you have read most of these stories over the years and changed most of them. Yes, Jamie, years. I don't know how many, but the number is above two. Your support and commitment to preserving my voice has been steady. It helps that you have a strong voice of your own.

Well, Patricia Jarvis, my partner of over 40 years, you read, commented, suffered, enjoyed and supported me through all of it. You are in the dedication. You belong there, carrying my heart with you.

INTRODUCTION

"Why should anyone read these stories?" After all, I haven't done anything particularly noteworthy in my life. Nor am I famous or writing about famous people. The stories were written while trying to understand my own life from the vantage of having lived over 70 years—within a year of 80 now, which is hard to believe. The task was emotional, intellectual, and serious, as it likely is for other aging people. It is best if our life reviews have positive outcomes. Luckily, that is how I feel, despite having reservations about leaving some things undone.

I looked for the meaning behind stories and poems and what they told me about life from an early age. So, when Dylan Thomas wrote: "Time held me green and dying though I sang in my chains like the sea," in 'Fern Hill,' for example, my life changed. There wasn't anything morbid about this; I just became intellectually aware that the greenness and death Thomas was talking about applied to me. I didn't think about death all the time, but it became a distant part of my life. The difference between then and now is that, somewhere in my late 60s or early 70s, I didn't just know of my impending death intellectually, but I knew about it emotionally, too.

Presenting this book is accompanied by feelings of humility and gratitude for the life I have been offered. Some things are going more slowly now, like day-to-day chores. I'm apt to find myself staring off into space or switching to do something else. Other things are moving far more rapidly, especially time. A desire to learn remains with a slowly developing willingness to have fun and joke around. A desire to teach is unavoidable, having taught, but it isn't solid, and it is pretty dominated by what I don't know. There is a far more vital need to withdraw and instruct myself. I hope the feeling isn't as selfish as I think it might be. It will be up to you to find anything of value here and make it fit yourself.

The stories begin with very early experiences and follow a roughly chronological order, which means some readers might find a sense of personal development in them. The roughness of the chronology comes from the fact that some are put together using thoughts, feelings, and events that happened over many years. All were chosen because they contained a lesson for me. The lessons may be small, prominent, or obscure. And, at times, there was more than one. Of course, you as a reader might already know what the events mean. Hopefully, you will still be entertained. If your luck as a reader is in, you may see something in your own life in a slightly different way. If you are fortunate, you might experience something new or have a new thought. If any of these things happen, then together, we have recreated what has been done for me. And I have paid part of the debt I owe to those who have preceded me.

– Fredrick J. Madryga, Ph.D.
August 20, 2021

SILENT STALKERS

The canyon we were living in had a great river running through it. The mountain ranges containing it surrounded us. They were so close they were overwhelming. The conifers covering their sides were dense, hiding mysteries. The unknown of the mountains and fishing in the creek that ran into the river fascinated me.

There was a tiny village we could easily walk to for food and other supplies. The store had sinkers, fishhooks, and nylon fishing line we could buy. One time I saw a small sturgeon the proprietor had caught lying in a wheelbarrow half full of water waiting to be cooked that evening. It was still circulating water through its gills. There was always something interesting at the store.

The village used to be a lot bigger when the gold rush passed through. One book said the Spanish, who had come up the Pacific coast, also came up the river as far as where we were living. They came much earlier than the prospectors panning for gold and the Chinese working on the railroad, who also panned for gold to send back to their homes. They weren't the first by any means. Lord only knows how long the First Nations had been there. Estimates in recent years suggest near 14,000 years in some places.

The road and train tracks following the river and passing through where we lived went west down to the Pacific coast over 100 miles away. They came back to go east far enough to disappear into places I didn't know. The trains had steam engines. We could hear the sound of their whistles when they were coming from the east through the canyon. It was harder to hear them coming from the west. Hearing a whistle, we would run down to the station to see the train come in. Sometimes it would hit one of the bantam chickens even after blowing its whistle. The bantams were constantly running and pecking around the station, and the train would squash them flat when it ran over them. There was nothing quite as flat as a banty run over by a train. I was fascinated and repulsed at the same time.

The road was an old wagon road. It was narrow and ran through steep country. There were cliffs where one stopped and pressed the car horn. A honk back meant you should wait until the approaching car passed by. I remember when my grampa worked on the road while it was being widened, and I recall the 1948 flood where the Fraser River almost reached the road and tracks where we lived. The reserve on the other side of the tracks disappeared overnight, though no one drowned.

I don't know if the one-room school where the First Nations kids took me is still there. Being only five years old, I sat at the back of the class near the heater. I guess they didn't want me to get cold. One day we all fed the old horse in the schoolyard from the apple tree at the back of the school. You may not believe me, but it ate so much that it fell over. A man had to come and put a tube in its side. I can still hear the gas escaping. The horse was OK, but we didn't feed it much anymore.

My father worked in Vancouver and drove up to see our family. It would take him over four hours to get to where we were living in the canyon. He started teaching me to fish when I was four by casting the line out and letting me reel it back in. Now, at five years old, I could fish on my own, and I chopped kindling for the stove that cooked our food while keeping us warm. Chopping the kindling wasn't hard. I held the hatchet blade on top of a piece of wood and hit the other end of the wood on the chopping block. So, no fingers were chopped off, and no leg was hit due to the short handle. Dad told me that a hatchet was the most dangerous axe because of the short handle. It could miss the chopping block and hit your leg.

Grampa showed me how to use a hammer to bang in nails. I could pound them into the cement step at the back door, which fascinated him. He also nearly broke his neck, falling over me when he carried lumber out the door and didn't see me working there. It was then that I learned about cussing.

There were other things that made life hard for Grampa, too. Tiny, their Corgi dog, was crazy about chasing skunks. One day, I saw Grampa start running toward the garden. Tiny, the skunk she was running after, and Grampa, who saw the skunk and was chasing Tiny, all arrived in the garden at the same time. The skunk, though upset, was fine as it trundled off into the bush with its tail still raised. But a lot of tomato juice was used on Grampa and Tiny to treat the effects of skunk blast. It didn't seem to work all that well. There were many cuss words, and Tiny's life was threatened more than once during the cussing.

Grandma was quiet. She usually stayed in the background, canning salmon, cooking, and cleaning the house. She kept everything clean. "You could eat off her floors," as one used to say. She was kind to me, but her quietness made her seem distant, and I don't remember her ever hugging me.

One memory I have of her is very discordant. I was pretty young when she killed a fly for landing on an ashtray that she had just washed. I don't know if the wetness slowed the fly down, but I can still see her gnarled, arthritic fingers closing on it and crushing its life out. It was an act so shockingly different from her apparent gentle nature that it attached itself to my memory of her. I came to wonder about her true nature and the life she had led. Later, I found out she had come from England to Canada as an indentured labourer. She had also gone through a world depression and a world war, as grampa had. Grandma even seemed distant from him.

"Glad to see you come, glad to see you go," she said to me the last time I visited her before she died. There were secrets in her life and the life of my other grandmother, too. I will never know what those secrets were, though I can guess.

It was my mother that I helped spill water down the hill behind our place during the winter. Carrying the buckets was hard work, but the water ran down the bank and froze. We could then go tobogganing using a broken flat shovel to sit on while holding the broken handle in front of us. Mom loved adventures and could do most things. She loved her children and all other children. Years later, she worked taking care of children born deformed and hidden away in a building. She didn't care about skin colour, size, degree of deformity, or handsomeness. She just loved kids.

There aren't enough pages in any book for a man to describe his mother. I knew her beautiful soul but wouldn't appreciate her adventurousness, courage, and competence until reaching my 50s. It was too late then; she had been injured, and I couldn't take her hunting with me in the north.

This was my external world, and many things were happening in it. The mountains enclosed me. My days were filled with adventures and mysteries. I didn't understand things like Mother's fear of losing me or my grandmother's secrets; such understanding would come much later. I simply experienced each thing that happened. And, in my unaware state, I continued slowly developing my inner world.

One day, I snuck away fishing. Poor Mom — I often did this, even though doing so led to a scolding and a slap on the seat of my pants. Her love of adventures didn't extend to me going to the creek by myself. She was afraid that I would fall in, hit my head on a rock, and drown. Mom never struck me hard enough to hurt me, but the message was delivered just the same. (She would hit me harder if I took my brother with me. He was only two-and-a-half years old and still a toddler.) Despite it all, I just knew there would be a trout in the pool below the house. What was a five-year-old boy to do? We always ate the trout I brought home, too. What was a mother to do?

Hiding my small fishing rod wasn't easy, but I managed to stash it near the root cellar dug into the bank on the trail to the creek, which was a further 30 or 40 feet below. An adult would disappear on the track when they reached the root cellar. So, mom wouldn't see me if I could get that far. All I had to do after digging worms was wait for my chance. The path was narrow and steep. It was crowded with deciduous trees where the conifers had been removed for lumber. The trail ended at a small ledge about six feet above the creek where I left my worms.

After scrambling down the rest of the way to the creek, I started fishing. A trout promptly took the worm while leaving the hook. It was not an unusual occurrence. I happily scrambled back up to the ledge and pulled another juicy worm from the can. Then, looking below to position my feet and go back down, I saw water running just below my sneakers. Shocked into immobility, I resisted the urge to step. The creek had risen three feet in the time it took me to go the six feet up to the ledge. Intent upon getting another worm and going back to fishing, I hadn't heard it come up. My immobility changed to a frantic scramble to get up onto the ledge. And I sat there watching the water running by. It was dirty and moving very fast as it ate at the steep bank below me. I could hear hissing sounds from the riffles

4

where big rocks were now hidden beneath its surface.

Mother's fears about falling in, hitting my head, and drowning became real. There is little doubt that the creek would have swept me away if I hadn't gone up the bank. I knew enough not to step back down. And, from my rapid scramble onto the ledge, it was clear I was frightened. Nature had warned me, and the image of that silent rise of water has remained indelible. It didn't stop me from sneaking away, though. My forays went farther and farther upstream, pursuing the mystery of the creek and wilderness as well as the fishing. But now I knew that water could change and sneak up on me, and I watched the stream differently.

On another day, I snuck out of a window very early in the morning to search for interesting rocks and to fish for trout. It had rained overnight. Drips from the trees were making a pattering sound in the moist air. The pathway I was following beside grampa's flume had puddles on it. I remember being worried that the water might be high and spoil the fishing. The creek did sound a bit high. In the terrible innocence of childhood, I was happier when conditions deprived the trout of food and places to hide, making it easier to catch them.

Seeing the ground was disturbed near one of the puddles, I went to look. The tracks of a large cat impressed in the mud were unmistakable. It was following the flume in the same direction I was. Bending to look more closely, I watched the water slowly breaking down the sides of one impression. He was a heavy cat, and his paw marks were deep. He was also very close as the water was just starting through the sides of his tracks. Carefully looking around, I couldn't see him, and I was afraid to go on. Encouraged by the rock hammer I was carrying in my little pack, however, I finally decided to continue.

The pool I was heading for was below a beautiful fall about 10 or 15 feet high. There was a ledge of rock that I fished from at one side of the fall. It projected into the deep water at its base, allowing excellent access to where the turbulence caused by its drop began to settle out. Not all accesses were so easy. A nice back-eddy swirled around the end of the rock, and the trout would hang there waiting for food. If the big cat came after me while I was fishing, I thought I could jump into the water and hit it with my hammer if it swam out to me. 'Ignorance is bliss,' as the old saying goes.

Reaching my fishing spot, I couldn't hear much because of the roaring of the fall. I felt uneasy at first. But there were many trout, and, as I fished, thoughts of the cat slowly receded from my awareness. Then, suddenly, the hair went up on the back of my neck. I became frightened and confused and began looking around. What had set me off? For a moment, I thought I saw a movement on the top of the thirty, or forty-foot bank behind me. Continuing to stare, I then saw action out of the corner of my eye. It was the cougar. He was running across a huge windfall stretched across the creek at the top of the falls. Smoothly stopping in the middle of the log in a partial crouch, he turned his head to look at me. Time seemed to stop. I don't know how long he stared. It was as if a magnifying glass had enlarged his face enough for his eyes to look right into mine. Who knows what was behind those eyes? He was utterly alien and the wildest thing I had ever seen. All that existed was that face with its staring eyes. I stayed frozen in place, feeling and hearing nothing. Then, in a flash, he was gone. Time began running, and I started breathing again.

Putting my rod down but keeping the rock hammer, I found a way up the bank to look at the flats where the first movement had occurred. The cougar's tracks circled near the edge of the bank. It looked like it had walked back and forth several times. Who knows what it was thinking as it was there watching me? Maybe it was wondering if I was good to eat? I was about the right size for a meal. Or, perhaps it saw the fish on the rock beside me and was thinking of coming down to get them? Whatever the case might be, the memory of the cougar would stay with me. I knew from its wild look that the cat could sneak up and eat my fish or me. While walking home, there were now two things in my inner world that could silently stalk me. And both were dangerous.

THE CHANGE

The river is large and opaque. Even in its calm moments, one can never completely trust it. A lot is going on beneath the surface. A riffle or an eddy might appear, stay for a while, then disappear. Occasionally a hidden piece of wood, or even a full-sized log, will explode unexpectedly to the surface. Sometimes you can see the pale belly of a dead fish or some other dead thing close to the surface. When a person understands the river, visions of prehistoric sturgeon can appear. They lie in the cold blackness, on a mound of muck at the base of a back eddy, raking in and devouring anything presented by the invisible currents. It is an entirely amoral place down there, an alien, atavistic world. Of course, I wasn't thinking of these things while the men talked to my father in grampa's yard.

They were great dark shapes, with deep rumbling voices, standing around my father as I held his leg. I could feel tension scarcely held in check by the sounds. It gripped them all. Young as I was, I could feel remember my father's leg flexing as they talked. I may not have understood it, but my body responded with flexing of its own. A woman had disappeared from the village. She was my playmate's mother, but I didn't know that. The men had their dogs with them, and, from the way things worked out, they probably wanted my father to bring ours. Of course, my father agreed. Looking back, there seemed little choice for any of them except to bring their dogs. What else could they do?

There is an interlude in which we were running. I often didn't see the things that hit my face or body. My father, running flat out for much of it, carried me in his arms while trying to protect me. Sometimes he put me down, letting me run for a bit, then picked me back up. I probably held them up too much. I could hear the wind rushing into my father's chest as he and the men around us put out... hard. Looking back, there was a sense of emergency and fear. A cycle of run, stop, then start running again had begun. It continued for a long time. I can remember hearing the gasping and panting when we stopped. The men bent over with their hands on their knees. The dogs were circling us, barking excitedly. Eventually calming down, they sat panting with their tongues hanging out. At one point, we started up, and the dogs began milling around. They quickened, and we changed direction, going faster as the pressure on us increased.

We had been following the flume grampa had built into the mountains for water, but we were now following closer to the creek as it went down toward the river. I could hear the water moving over the rocks, and I remember seeing the place near the creek where the First Nations women left me fish roe wrapped in leaves after cleaning salmon. Then, everything changed again. The men stopped pushing so hard. They became tentative. Perhaps they were starting to accept what they feared. I'll never know, but whatever was going on was still powerful.

Looking back, I feel a sense of inevitability. Perhaps I am manufacturing the feeling, but it is natural to me nevertheless and will remain so. I can remember the shock when we arrived. There was silence.

We must have been going much of the night before we reached the river. How else could I remember the light being the silvery light of dawn? Before us was a trail of footprints in the sand. The light outlined the edges of those prints and drove opaque shadows into their depths. They had a terrible finality to them as they went to the bank of the river, stopping and not coming back. What had happened was irrevocable, undeniable. Confirming all our fears, they demanded our acceptance. The men stood and smoked, saying nothing while looking at those tracks, and I watched them. The dogs sat and panted, staying with the men, not following the tracks to the bank.

It was the first time I sensed something happened to women those grown men didn't understand. It scared them, and I felt their fear. Somehow my young boy's mind knew the words 'change of life,' I believed this made her crazy and caused her to drown herself in the river. I can't tell you how I knew this, but I did. It's possible I heard the men saying it at the river that morning and filled in the blanks later on. Or maybe I heard other adults talking. I can't remember. Years later, I asked both my parents about the death, and they confirmed that people believed the change to be the cause. So, my playmate's mother exists alone in my young boy's mind, without understanding or help.

Lament

You come back to me from your journey, my friend's mother, a sister in a primeval place. And sometimes tears spring to my eyes. You come alone during quiet times. I can see your body turning slowly in the currents. You are wrapped in the chill and darkness of the river's waters. It is like a ballerina's slow, powerful dance, light but inevitable, even wild at times. Occasionally you put a pale spot on the surface of the water as your body turns against the terrible darkness below. I grieve how you left and for the interruption of your journey at the bridge many miles downstream. For two weeks, you had travelled in the dark driven by the currents through the twists in the river's course. Perhaps your journey continued despite the bridge. But I could not follow you, and vestiges of my fear are still there to be re-awakened.

REX

Rex was a rather large, good-hearted, black Labrador Retriever who was friendly with just about everyone he met. On my more dispassionate days, I am forced to admit that he wouldn't win prizes in a dog contest like a million other black labs. Nevertheless, Rex had many of the excellent characteristics of the breed. He was not particularly smart, but he was willing to swim at any time, just about anywhere, with or without the need to retrieve anything. He was 'up' for just about any adventure and loved to go hunting and fishing. He still holds a special place in my heart even after viewing him through the rippled glass of many years. Being still in my teen years when we met, I had no idea of the lessons Rex would teach me. We approached each of our adventures with full hearts, unfettered by the weight of many years. If you had tried to tell me where our relationship would go or how serious it would become near the end, I would not have known how to react. Even with the distortion of years, some parts of our story remain challenging to believe. Perhaps the truth of it all was concealed by the fact that Rex could be such a goof, albeit a humorous one, on occasion. His reaction to a ground squirrel provides a case in point.

Rex spotted the squirrel while we were walking along the train tracks. It wasn't a particularly impressive squirrel and not the first he had ever spotted. As was usual, Rex, who had some form of sliding scale for judging these matters, seemed to feel it was one of the finest squirrels he had ever encountered. Seeing a possible playmate, he immediately took off at warp speed to introduce himself. Meanwhile, viewing Rex on a diminishing approach vector, the ground squirrel quickly disappeared under a pile of railroad ties stacked neatly beside the tracks. Arriving soon after the disappearance of his potential friend, Rex jammed his nose under the pile and, with tail elevated and wagging, began digging frantically.

Perhaps there was something special about this squirrel. It had mapped its avenue of retreat long before Rex had shown up and soon popped out the other side of the pile. I thought it would continue by exiting into the safety of the bushes, but it had other ideas. Without a noticeable pause, the squirrel jumped onto the pile of ties. It was heading over to the side where Rex was digging. Looking down at him, it began chattering fiercely. Not thinking to look above him to where the exciting sound effects were coming from, Rex continued digging with admirable resolve and increasing enthusiasm. Meanwhile, the squirrel, after scolding enough to vent its ire at having its day disrupted, popped off the pile and ran into the woods. Rex, raising his head at the cessation of the sound, began looking around. Appearing confused, he lowered his head, took a few sniffs at the hole he had dug, whined, and, after a few more tentative digs, ceased digging. I felt genuine love for the dog while looking at the puzzled expression on this homely mug as he was walking back to me. How could one not identify with his feelings about the mysterious and confusing world he lived in?

Rex's uniqueness also came out when we were hunting. Like most labs, he would almost turn himself inside-out if I picked up a shotgun. Seeing the gun in my hands, he would begin whining and wagging his tail hard enough to leave a bruise if it hit your leg. The slightest additional suggestion that we might be going hunting— almost any movement was suggestion enough—would increase his intensity. Launching himself toward the door, then standing with his body rigid and his nose in the crack, he would wait briefly, often whining softly. If I wasn't preparing to leave fast enough, he would begin rapidly cycling back and forth between me and the door while whining loudly. I confess that I occasionally picked up my shotgun just to watch this performance. If I decided not to go hunting, gloom would descend, and I would have to pet him while making promises about going out later. Perhaps, on the occasions when I picked up the shotgun without going hunting, we were teaching ourselves how to get over the disappointment. There was usually some kind of lesson in my experiences with him.

Things appeared to be progressing along typical lines during one hunt. Rex had gone through his preliminary work-up after seeing me pick up the shotgun. Now, he was happily ranging far enough ahead to ensure I would be unable to hit a grouse if it appeared. I was following him in my usual state of semi-watchfulness to wave goodbye when the grouse flew. After about half an hour of pleasantly ambling along in this fashion, I noticed him standing under a conifer tree, looking upward. His uniqueness as a hunter was coming to the fore.

Having it on good authority that grouse do, indeed, sit in trees, I believed Rex was trying to tell me about the presence of one in the tree. Shotgun in ready position, I began my stalk. Seeing me coming, Rex started sneaking glances at me while accelerating his tail, wagging and increasing the rate of the soft whining sound he was making. Still emitting the occasional soft whine and restive body movement, he stayed by my side when I reached him and continued looking up the tree with me. Who knows how long we gazed into that tree? Despite our diligence, however, we couldn't see any grouse, and we were eventually forced to stand down.

I'm reluctant to admit it, but we followed the same scenario with the same results on two more occasions: Rex looking up. Me looking up. No grouse looking down. My enthusiasm was wearing a little thin when Rex began looking up the fourth tree. Comforted by the fact we were alone, I did go over and look up the tree with him, but not for very long. Rex, who likely had some questions of his own by this time, didn't seem disturbed to quit early, either. A few steps after resuming our walk, I chose a tree myself and began looking. Pausing briefly, Rex walked over and started looking up the tree with me. Wishing I had a tail to wag, I found that he would even make a whining sound on his way over if I whined while sneaking looks back at him. Who knows what was behind it all?

From that day forward, either one of us could initiate an up-the-tree-grouse-looking game. I can't speak for Rex, but I never did see a grouse up any of the trees he and I scrutinized together. For a while, I blamed Rex's unique behaviour on the old Greek fellow—a specialist in hunting robins for the dinner table—who trained him as a young dog. But there were not any robins in those trees. Believe me; I looked for them.

During one of our fishing trips, things between Rex and me took on a more serious note. The trip began with a problem. A back-eddy drove our boat into a rock hidden under the water's surface. The blow was hard enough to break the shear pin on the outboard motor. Not having a spare pin, we were looking at a three-mile hike to get home. Luckily, however, we were close to the mouth of the creek when the accident happened. So, after a certain amount of judicious paddling, we succeeded in getting off the river into the creek's mouth.

Beginning with an accident might sound like a significant event, but a little walk never concerned me all that much. I don't recall such incidents ever interfering with fishing, either. At its worst, the mishap might require my father to go downriver with our neighbour and his boat to pull ours back home. They would wear the same dour expressions while doing this that they had on the other occasions in which they had bailed us out. Their wilderness code, and the fact they wouldn't want to lose my father's boat, ensured they would make the trip. The punishments they would mete out would not be fatal, amounting mainly to some gnashing of teeth and the making of the odd quiet threat. So, resolving the problem of the injured boat, we left it tied up at the mouth of the creek and began walking upstream fishing.

Rex showed his usual helpfulness by walking ahead of me to scrutinize the pools. He was especially careful to walk into any that reeked of fish to ensure trout were present. No doubt, he wanted to prevent me from wasting my time. The trout, of course, taking exception to the intrusion, were nowhere to be found. It was a familiar issue between us and one in which Rex felt I exhibited a severe lack of understanding concerning his motives. Not having learned that if one kept doing the same thing, one would experience the same results, I soon began yelling and swearing at him. To my shame, I even went as far as hurling small rocks toward him. Rex, obviously frustrated by his inability to educate me concerning pool selection in fishing, and confused by my blatantly unjust behaviour, took off on a tour of his own.

Continuing upstream while happily catching trout in the now undisturbed pools, I eventually started missing Rex's company and began listening for his return. On previous trips, he would come back from time to time, or one would hear him barking, but there hadn't been a peep out of him for the longest time. We were in a wild country, and my concern for him started building. After reflecting on how he had always come through before, however, I decided to continue fishing while keeping one ear open to hear him when he was coming back

The stream we were fishing was moving fast as it lost elevation on its way to the river. It came through sheer cliffs at one point, creating a waterfall nearly fifteen feet high. One side of the fall was against a sheer wall and impassible. The side I was on had a vertical cliff face with a small ledge or bench that would allow me to get above the falls. A massive tree had landed against the shelf at one time, ending up pressed against the face of the cliff part way down. The tree was barely close enough, but I was able to chin myself up onto the ledge from it and continue fishing.

After a delightful interlude of wading and walking gravel banks while catching fish, I noticed that the shadows on the mountains and trees had moved a fair distance, and I began walking downstream. Eventually reaching the ledge and hanging from its edge, I dropped the few remaining inches to stand on the windfall. Then, leaning against the cliff-face to have a rest, I heard a sound above me. Looking up, Rex was standing on the bench, looking down at me. He must have run entirely around the mountain on his journey. There wasn't any other way for him to get to where he was. And it had taken him several hours to get there. Now he was stuck, and we would arrive home in darkness if he went back the way he had come.

We were in a serious fix. Not only were we losing light, but I had also left a note saying where we were going and when we would be back. Failing to make a deadline was a situation taken very seriously at home, let alone failing to return after it became dark. After making our way down the creek, Rex and I would have a three-mile hike ahead of us. Many dangers would confront those who would come looking for us, too. We had to get Rex down off that ledge. He couldn't jump down, and it wasn't going to be easy getting him off it in any other way. The more I looked at the situation, the more challenging the problem seemed to become.

For one thing, Rex would have to step down onto my shoulders while I was on the windfall. In doing so, he would be over-extending his body and committing his weight entirely to my control. That was the crux of the matter and a lot to ask of any dog. I would also be forced to carry his 80 pounds—he was all of that—while shuffling backward down the windfall. I wasn't sure that I would be able to turn around, and thought moving down while not looking at where we were going would markedly increase the danger.

The windfall was slippery with spray from the creek. We could easily fall. It was virtually certain to happen if Rex struggled, and injury to one or both of us was likely. If we lost our balance, I might be able to throw Rex into the creek, which could save him. But I would have to deal with the water-slick rocks waiting for me, seven or eight feet below. Despite the fearfulness of what could be ahead of us, it looked like he would have to step down.

Extending my arms up the cliff with a feeling of dread, I rested my hands as close to the top of the ledge as I could and began patting my right shoulder with my left hand. Damned if he didn't get it! Whining and lowering his body, he belly-crawled forward to the edge, then extended a paw to my shoulder. Then, whining even louder, he pulled back and stood up. I remained in place while patting my shoulder and saying encouraging things to him. He kept complaining and moving from side to side. Instead of leaving to go back around the mountain, however, he crept back and, after a false start or two, we managed to get his paws on my shoulders.

I remember slowly moving my left hand behind his legs, then following with my right. Lifting his legs up and toward me, we were able to transfer his weight onto my shoulders and hands. We managed to ease his bum past the edge of the bench from that point. Then, lowering Rex to a more comfortable position, my search began for a way to turn. Leaning one hip against the cliff face, then turning my feet by tiny bits with my hip following, we managed to achieve a position facing down the windfall. With the roar of the falls in my ears and the fine mist from it hitting my face, we then leaned against the cliff face for a brief rest. Holding Rex securely, I would have liked to stay there, but we still had to get down that log.

All the time we were getting off the ledge, turning on the windfall, and resting, I could feel tremors running through Rex's body. They continued as we shuffled down that slippery log, but he didn't struggle. We would never have made it if he had not controlled himself. The lesson seemed straightforward enough. In his world, you trust your friends, and if someone trusts you, you don't let them down. I knew such values and experiences could be potentially dangerous, but they didn't feel life-threatening. Looking back, however, it is true that we could have been killed.

I was approaching 20 years old when my parents asked me to come and take care of their place. It was then that my need for a smoke put Rex and me in peril again. I had seen him from time to time since our adventure fishing the creek, but dogs age more quickly than humans, and he now looked older while sporting a classic grey muzzle. We were happy to see each other, but he was getting arthritic, and we couldn't wrestle like we used to. He had still shown some interest when I picked up my shotgun, but there wasn't the drama in it there had been on earlier occasions.

My parents had left on their trip during the spring melt. The river was extremely high. Its power and speed were incredible, and much debris was coming downstream. One would hardly know the giant whirlpool, which was some distance downriver from where we lived, was present during low water. But it was massive in such flooding. On one occasion, I recall seeing a barn roof pulled entirely under the surface by the whirlpool and coming up in pieces further down the river.

As you can imagine, the situation was not ideal for going across the river. But being a typical smoker who has run out of cigarettes, I decided to go and get more—it is hard to over-estimate the dedication of smokers to their habit. Knowing Rex would want to come, I put him in Dad's shop and shut the door to keep him from following me.

While tying the boat up near the road after crossing the river, I heard one of the two guys who had been watching me come over say: "Hey, look at that dog." My heart almost stopped. It had to be Rex. I must have failed to close the door to the shop properly. That damned latch was always sticky. Why had I been in such a hurry? Turning to look, there he was, trying to swim across the river, confirming all my worst fears. He had swum the river before but never during such a massive flood. He was older now, too. He made it just past the halfway mark before I saw him lose his way and begin circling. Age and the flood had caught up to him. He was still fighting, but he was riding lower and lower in the water as the current carried him down the river toward that giant whirlpool. It would deliver the coup de grace, and he would drown.

My going out to get Rex was the irrational act of a young man. Not only was there massive power and speed in the river, along with rapids and debris, but it was almost certain we would end up in the whirlpool. Was a fifteen-horsepower outboard enough to power out or even get me to Rex in time? Lord, how I wished it was a twenty! I didn't even know how to get him into the boat without swamping. On the plus side, he was only about 60 or 70 pounds now, and I had a life jacket. As I got into the boat, I thought about that fishing trip. In his innocence and loyalty, Rex would come back for me if our roles were reversed. With a feeling of fatalism and knowing we would only get one chance; I started the motor to go out and get him. I was terrified.

I planned to drop below Rex, then moving up river against the current, or, if my luck was in, holding in it, I would pick him up on his way by. He still had a heart as big as a mountain, but he was just about all in when he saw me coming toward him. With only his head showing, he quit fighting the current and began trying to get to the boat. I remember being afraid that he would not make it, or I would fail to catch him, or I would misjudge and hit him with the boat. Things were just a blur of tears and sweaty fear. Somehow, I managed to snag his collar along with a fist full of his fur and flesh on his way by. Combined with my hold on him, the vicious current threw him out of the water and toward the boat. Could it be that all four of his paws were pulled tightly to his body in the 'puppy being carried position' as he came out of the water? It is what I remember seeing. Luckily for us, the trajectory of the boat upstream, combined with the current rushing past us and the insanely panicked strength of my pull, lifted Rex just high enough to make him hit the top of the boat's side. My grip was barely strong enough to allow him to roll into the boat before it failed, and I dropped him.

In all the action, the boat swapped ends; no doubt this also helped get Rex into the boat, but I was unaware of it. A big wave rolled entirely over me, driving the motor and stern downward. Blinded by the dirty water, I remember feeling how cold it was, and, though it may be hard to believe, I also recall thinking that we might have a chance if the motor was still running when it came up. By some miraculous intervention from on high, the engine did come up, and it was still running. As the wave subsided and my eyesight came back, I was now looking downriver in the direction of the whirlpool. I saw Rex lying at the bottom of the boat in about four inches of water. He had an embarrassed expression on his face while looking at me. His tail was thumping and splashing apologetically as it hit the water and the side of the boat.

The sun in the sky was brighter when the motor was still running after its dunking. But we were heading toward the whirlpool, and it looked every bit as bad as I thought it would. Feeling the beginning of its pull, I throttled just hard enough to turn the boat into, and slightly across, the powerful primary current of the river. Luckily, the motor was strong enough to overcome the early pull from the whirlpool. Being careful to use just enough power without losing control of the boat by jumping the engine out of the water, I continued maneuvering across the current. After getting to the other side, it was easy enough to pick up a back eddy and begin our way upstream. It will comfort any true smokers to know that we then crossed the river to get my pack of cigarettes at the village store despite being soaked with dirty water. The two watchers on the bank of the river said nothing as I walked by them, pretending to be unaffected by all that had happened.

Looking back, I can still see Rex lying there in the boat after we tied up. We were both drying off. I had opened the stern evacuation plug to eject the water on our way back across the river. Rex's head was up, and his paws were in front of him. The sun was hitting one side of his grey muzzle. I loved him, and my heart almost broke as I saw how old and gaunt he looked. I couldn't know while looking at him that this would be our last trip together. He looked happy. If another adventure were to have offered itself, he would have gone with me.

THE KILLER

The impression of a vast, primeval beast from some dark fantasy was inescapable in the darkness. When I first saw it, it had scattered lights hanging on its black form as it loomed over me and everything around me. It made mysterious, disturbing, even frightening sounds that varied in loudness. There were smells suggesting things like blood, offal, and unknown substances. It was a cloying, warm, oddly viscid smell that stuck to my clothes. Bad, fearful things could happen here.

We were doing some long overdue maintenance jobs and building new structures in the beast. My boss, who owned the construction outfit I was working for, was exploring its catacombs to see if there was work to be done there. The area we were in was long, narrow, and dark. It was quiet, and sometimes we would hear muffled sounds coming from above us. Weak light came from an occasional small lightbulb hanging from the ceiling. There were obsolete or broken pieces of equipment pushed up against the walls. They swam into view as we approached each light. The equipment looked like it had been forgotten for many years. We couldn't tell what the pieces were for because each was obscured by three or four inches of rancid fat. A narrow ditch covered by a sturdy metal grating built into the concrete floor ran beside us as we walked slowly along. The muffled sounds from above us changed, and the ditch beside us began running with fluid. I could smell blood but couldn't see it until we were beside one of the lights. The stream was several inches deep in the bottom of the ditch. It shone a dirty pinkish colour in the weak light. I can remember hoping we wouldn't find work as we walked on. There was a feeling of horror that one could not get away from.

There were many things to be afraid of in my surroundings. At 15 years of age and on my first real job, I'm sure I didn't know all of them, and I certainly didn't understand most of them. Two of the men I was working with were part of it. Seeing its structure at night, and being in its catacombs, was the beginning.

The Beast was a slaughterhouse, and we had to do our work at night to keep things clean. Slaughtering was done during the day. Giant tarps had been put over the large entryways to our worksite. They prevented dust caused by the renovations we were doing from spreading to other rooms in the complex. Everything was made from cement and metal in the killing and butchering rooms. The floors and ceilings of both were made of reinforced cement. There were rows of metal tables with tops of cinder mix lined up in the butchering area. Steel runners, located above the tables, had large hooks attached to pulleys running along with them. Later, I saw dead animals hung on those hooks while travelling down the rows of tables. People in overalls were standing on top of the tables with knives making various cuts as they went by. Horrendous though the process may have been, it gave the impression of efficiency and lack of waste. Urine and offal from the cadavers were hosed into the sewer my boss and I had seen in the catacombs. The sewer ended in the river near the slaughterhouse, where fish congregated to eat bits carried by the outfall. (It was an excellent place to fish.) Even the smallest piece of flesh and the heads and organs appeared to have a use in the beast. The small pieces went into making sausage and wieners, which may explain the reluctance of some to eat such end products. I even saw a huge cart full of skinned pig heads that were set aside, though I never found out what they were used for (I guessed fertilizer of some sort.) The killing room, of course, provided the first step in processing.

One wall mated the killing room with the butchering section. The wall between the two regions was clad with steel. It didn't extend to the ceiling but had a large portal at the top that opened into the butchering area. There were chains travelling up the wall and through the gap at the top. There was a large, open tank of water beside the wall on the butchering side. I saw later that the water was hot and steaming when the rooms were operating. Our first job was jackhammering out the old tabletops and cement floors to build a new killing floor. Work would start at seven at night and end around six in the morning. The slaughterhouse would begin its business around eight after we had left.

One weekend, with the jackhammering finished, we worked straight through from Friday afternoon to Monday morning, moving debris out of the old rooms. We loaded the trash on a truck parked outside to take it to the city dump. I remember being surprised when they let me drive the dump truck, proud, too. Moving debris was acknowledged to be a shitty job, and the guys didn't even seem to mind my doing the driving. Maybe it was what they called my "shit-eating grin" that defused them. Driving the truck was a bit scary because of the chance of running into a cop. I was only 15 and didn't have a driver's license, let alone a license to drive a truck. Driving was a better job than picking up dirty pieces of cement and much more fun. Maybe it's best to tell you again that the crew itself wasn't as sweet as it might sound. Any pleasure I experienced while working in the place, or driving the truck, was intermixed with other feelings.

By this time, I knew that two of the men on the crew were rape artists. I use the word 'artists,' not in a good way, but to describe something else entirely. They worked as a team while picking up 'singletons' in their car. I found this out while they talked about what they would do with their time off one night. They saw I was listening as they discussed what they intended and where they planned to go.

"After all," they told me. "Who would believe a single female even if she decided to tell. None of them have told on us before. Besides, no one is being killed."

What they said was made to sound like they were re-assuring me. But saying no one was killed was an implied death threat—take my word for this. They made it clear that no one would believe me if I told, either. I doubt they killed the women, though. They were too much into control and too cunning to risk themselves. I couldn't see a way of getting rid of them being outgunned in every way. Any possibility I could come up with that might get rid of them would likely result in getting rid of myself. I was young, quite untutored in life, and simply didn't know what to do.

On the weekend following, we built wooden pathways and began pushing wheelbarrows of cement for the new floor and the tops of the tables. It felt good to fill the tops of the tables. The cinder mix we used was beautiful. It was light, making the load easy to control while wheeling and pouring. But the gravel mix for the floors was heavy. The pain began as soon as the cement poured into the wheelbarrow. The mix kept moving in the barrow knocking it from side to side while wheeling it down the narrow runways. I could barely control the load, and pouring it was even tougher than wheeling. I had to lift the handles on the wheelbarrow high against the heavily sloshing weight of the cement while keeping it from falling to one side or the other. There were times when I truly felt like giving up, especially during the late hours of the night when transporting that gravel mix seemed to go on forever. There was something exquisite about the torture from the back-and-forth motion of heavy cement while trying to lift and pour. The action of the cement seemed carefully designed to push me just to the brink of what I was capable of. But I was slowly toughening up and be damned if I would quit. Somehow, I made it through. Besides, the two 'artists' were watching my every move. Any weakness on my part might lead to dangerous outcomes.

While working such long hours, you become like an automaton. Life was loading, wheeling, dumping, and not much else. Dissociation blocked the pain to some extent. I hardly felt the effect of being surrounded by the slaughterhouse, but it was still a dark time. After that long weekend, when our work began to move outdoors, I started watching and thinking again. How the slaughterhouse worked slowly became more apparent. It was at that point that I became aware of the killer. There were two things behind my growing awareness; one was the lunchroom, and the other was the killing process.

Cattle were killed separately from pigs, sheep, and lambs. They were herded into a chute one at a time and moved forward until their head went through a collar. Using a gun mounted on a ball joint, a man placed the gun's barrel on each cow's forehead and shot it. The animals I saw shot dropped to the floor immediately. The carcass was lifted using a winch and metal hooks with an attached pulley. The pulley ran over the metal tracks I mentioned before, and people washed the carcass with hoses while it hung there. Then the pulley carried the dead animals down the steel runway, passing over the tables with the cinder mix tops. People standing on the tables holding various tools made cuts as the dead animal went by them.

The pigs, sheep, and lambs went to another killing room like the one we were re-building. The animals were connected to chains that lifted them by their hind legs against the metal-clad wall. The killer, who held a large, long-handled knife with a blade that curved back on itself, placed a diagonal cut in the animal's throat. The chains rapidly transported the bleeding, dying animal over the wall, dropping it into the hot bath on the other side. It was then suspended from hooks on the same metal runway that carried the cattle and went down what I had soon begun calling the tables of a thousand cuts.

The process evoked many negative feelings in me. I remember being struck by shock and revulsion when first seeing it. But I soon became desensitized to the point where I could watch the animals being butchered or herded into the killing area without feeling much at all. My desensitization was not perfect, however, and at times, the horror would leak through. Events would overcome dissociation, and other feelings and behaviours would break out. One such incident in which this happened involved a pig with a broken leg that was being herded to the killing room. As you might imagine, it was reluctant to go there, and the herder was hitting it with a stick. My boss leaped the fence and began beating him up. I followed right after my boss but noticed the herder had dropped his stick and wasn't defending himself. So, I stopped in confusion, and so did my boss. The two men stood there staring at each other. After talking quietly, the herder picked up his stick, and my boss returned to our job site. I never did find out what they said.

Events like that were rare exceptions to a generally smooth operation. I'm still amazed at how fast the process was and how ephemeral life can be. A hundred and fifty animals could go through that place in what seemed like no time at all. The animals had some sense of what was going on, especially the pigs and sheep. Their knowing was a significant part of the horror that occasionally broke into my consciousness and still is. (The knowledge that humans could be killed en masse in similar ways wasn't lost on me. It surfaced when I heard of a 'mercy' killing floor using gas that was being built in a slaughterhouse in Alberta.)

There is no getting around killing. After you have seen and done it, you either suppress it—those of you unconsciously eating hamburgers may take heart—or you learn to live with it in some way. It changes you, and whether you know it or not, we are all dealing with it in some way. My way was by starting to hunt and fish at a young age with my father. We didn't take more than we needed and ate what we killed. It made sense to me. Also, there can be a kind of innocence about being young. I don't believe I had the experience to be genuinely empathetic about many things during those early years, including the killing. But, my father, who accepted that killing was part of life while still being affected by it, raised me to face killing in a sensitive and pro-social way. Now, however, I was beginning to see the systematic things done each day on a mass scale to provide our food, and it bothered me.

I saw a rabbi inspect the processes in the slaughterhouse and bless the meat. Despite not being Jewish, I was comforted by his presence. It was wonderful that a group would accept responsibility for their food and how it was made. Nevertheless, my trouble with the environment I was in persisted, and I eventually began focussing on the killer. He stood there repeatedly taking life every day. Thinking about this made doubts and ambivalent feelings about him keep welling up in my mind and heart. In what way was he changed by what he did? Was he even human? In large part, the lunchroom set me up for what I was feeling.

The owner of the slaughterhouse built the lunchroom for the workers. It provided products from the slaughtered animals that employees could eat. I especially remember the milk and the steaks, but there were other things like sausages, wieners, and bread and butter to make sandwiches. It was a good spread. I recall thinking that what the slaughterhouse employees would choose to eat could provide some sort of recommendation for myself and others. The steaks were highly prized. The wieners and sausages disappeared more slowly. They did with me, too, though I still ate them. My boss and I were welcome to use the lunchroom after we finished pouring the new killing floor, and the rest of the crew had gone to another job. We stayed behind to do some further repair work and maintenance.

The slaughterhouse was old, and the organization of the lunchroom had become fixed over time. Long-term employees took most of the seats, and I ended up sitting beside one of the killers. The arrangement certainly facilitated the internal processes going on in me, though I hardly spoke to him. The killer was on the tall, slender side. He seemed a bit diminutive to me, an under-whelming kind of guy. It was as if his physical characteristics did not define him all that much. Maybe if he had a huge prognathic jaw or massive shoulders, it would have made a difference, but he didn't. I believe the killer came to exist almost as a symbol to me, rather than a real person, though I didn't quite understand just what the symbol meant. He looked like other people. He appeared to eat, dress, and talk like them. But could a person killing animals, day after day for 12 years, remain human and retain human feelings? The question stuck, as you can see. They talked about how long they had worked there one day and confirmed the length of time he had been doing his job. As chance would have it, an unusual event involving the killer gave me the beginnings of an answer to my question.

The event began when my boss and I had brought bag lunches. When an unexpected load of lambs came in, we were sitting outside eating. Where we sat overlooked the outside wall of the killing room, and we could see inside it over the outer gate. The room was usually inactive at lunchtime, which allowed us to ignore it. But with the truck's appearance, it became active, and the killer soon came into the killing space carrying his knife. Maybe I'm wrong about this, but it seemed as if continuing to sit there became an issue for my boss and me. Perhaps we felt the moral side of our souls required it. I'll never know. At any rate, we continued to sit there watching, with our sandwiches in hand.

Very quickly, about three or four lambs were placed in the chains, stuck, then lifted over the wall to be dropped into the hot bath on the other side. Suddenly, the killer fumbled a lamb, and it got away from him. It ran around the killing area baaing pathetically. Trapped in the small room, the lamb ran to the killer's leg leaning against it and rubbing its head up and down while continuing to baa frantically. The killer bent down and grabbed it, but the unimaginable happened. He fumbled it again while trying to put it into the chains. Predictably, the lamb ran, then did the very same thing it had before. Running over to the killer and pressing against his leg, it again began rubbing its head up and down repeatedly, all the while continuing to cry out. The killer looked down at it for a few seconds, then looking up and staring into space, he released the lamb. Turning toward the gate, he threw his knife into the corner of the room. Walking out of the room, he quietly closed the gate behind him and went out into the yard.

Another killer quickly appeared. I'm not even sure where he came from. He must have jumped over the outside gate, but I didn't see him do it. Picking up the knife, he moved quickly to finish the job. The moment exists in stasis in my mind. The situation would have probably unravelled into chaos if that new killer wasn't quick in carrying out what he had to do.

My boss and I stepped down from where we were sitting and turned our backs before the frightened lamb died, though we were both sure it did. I was thinking about what I had seen while we walked back to the truck, preparing to finish our day. We never talked about it, but I'm sure my boss, a decent man, was having his thoughts, too. The silence we were walking in was unusual. I felt sorry for the first killer and sad about the killing. I was also feeling happy he had thrown his knife into the corner. He was still human with human feelings. The decent side of his nature was still there, even after 12 years of taking life. It seems that I began to understand the sacrifices made to sustain our lives at that moment. It was a process with a tentative beginning, and, in this instance, the resilience of youth allowed me to move on to many other things. But the thoughts continued coming up over the years. They led toward the realization of how we often don't appreciate or acknowledge what is done for us as a society. How we don't see, or respect, the contribution made by the killers, or those others, who do all the shitty jobs. It took a long time for me to understand that terms such as 'redneck' and 'poor white trash' are what we use to defend ourselves against the sacrifices we force upon them by the society we've created.

RABBIT JUSTICE

No capon priest
was the Goodly Fere
But a man of men was he!
– Ezra Pound, "Ballad of the Goodly Fere"[1]

A savage place! as holy and enchanted
As e'er beneath a waning moon was haunted
By woman wailing for her demon lover
– Samuel Taylor Coleridge, "Kubla Khan"[2]

It was my friend Hugh who set me up to experience rabbit justice. He was a natural-born leader and one I had a hard time saying *no* to. His most recent brainstorm involved forming a bank for our class assignment in economics. It was not clear what part he would play in this, other than as a leader and 'idea' man. But it became evident, as he waxed poetic, that I would be the most logical person to find a way to finance the project. Like many bright ideas, Hugh's turned out to contain some truth. It worked a treat on paper and in our high school economics class. What happened on the bus when I was going home after trying to find a way of financing our project strikes me as truer to life. It was something I never mentioned to him. I don't know what he would have thought about what happened, and it is too late to ask him.

At first, riding home felt restful after spending several hours in the downtown library reviewing the records of many penny stocks. The bus was crowded but still picking up passengers. I was dozing in my seat in the sunshine when it pulled away from a stop and a young woman and young man made their way toward where I was sitting. Their appearance suggested they were together, but there was a worrisome, even scary, tension between them. The young woman

[1] New Directions, 1956.
[2] London: John Murray, 1816.

looked sullen, giving the impression that she had a problem, or was one. The young man following her was big, with an angry, dangerous look which worried me even more.

Running parallel to the sides of the bus, the seat I was sitting in provided a good vantage point to watch the two as they approached. It accommodated four people, like the one running parallel across the aisle from me. A single space was available beside an older man sitting across from me, and the sullen woman sat in it. Looking unassuming, a bit seedy, and wearing a grubby raincoat inappropriate for the weather, the old fellow had not impressed me much. So, apart from a glance when he got on the bus, I had pretty much ignored him. I did notice that he put a paper bag he was carrying on the floor beside his foot after sitting down.

Now, with the young woman sitting beside him and her threatening boyfriend looming over them, I had a second look at the old fellow. He still looked innocuous. Seeing him encircled by such an explosive couple, my mind elevated him to prey status by naming him The Rabbit. The feeling of threat in the scene was palpable. At this point, the tension was coming from potential rather than action. There may even have been a slight hiatus because the two lovebirds did not seem to be doing much.

Suddenly, what I had been worrying about happened. The young man hit The Rabbit in the face. It was a vicious assault, unprovoked, and shocking in its violence. The cause of the attack must have resided in the young man's head, whatever it was. Replaying the scene in my mind, I can see the older man recoiling back, bouncing off the seat. When The Rabbit fell, he landed on his side with his face hitting softly on the floor. It struck me at the time that the strength of his recoil and how quickly he went back might be because, like an experienced fighter, he rode the blow.

We did not make eye contact, but I saw that his eyes were open. He appeared aware of things around him while lying there and was allowing himself time to recover. Subsequent events suggest he also decided what he would do while staying down.

A worker, who was also physically well set up, had come out of his seat after the blow had landed on The Rabbit. Swearing and grabbing the boyfriend, he kept shaking him while calling for someone to get the cops. I'm sure all of us who had seen what happened were in sympathy with what he was shouting but, as it turned out, he was also providing cover for what was going on elsewhere.

For some reason, I had fixed my gaze on what The Rabbit was doing and heard the workman's shouting some distance in the background. Others on the bus were watching the worker and the young man while the shaking was happening. I saw The Rabbit roll weakly back and forth while making feeble efforts to get up. There was some blood coming out of his nose, and I remember thinking, in a distant way, that one might expect more blood than there was.

The Rabbit began mumbling: "No. No. No."

Hearing him, I had the strangest impression that he was trying to tell the worker not to harm the young man who had assaulted him. After several false starts, while muttering all the way, The Rabbit finally began to get somewhere. Reaching out with one arm and grabbing the seat he had been sitting upon, he arrived at a crouched position. Then, his other hand reached for the brown paper bag he had placed near his leg. In all the excitement, I had forgotten that brown bag. Now, as it swam into view, I watched him gripping it tightly and sat holding my breath. His subsequent movements were poetry.

Uncoiling off the floor, The Rabbit drove his body upward in a compact circular movement which put the full force of his legs, hips, and arms behind the bag he was now swinging. Watching the bag as it travelled, I saw it hit the young man who had assaulted him in the face. It was a magnificent blow. A wound magically appeared, penetrating the bridge of the young man's nose and splitting his cheeks open on both sides. Blood gushed forth and began running down the floor of the bus. Broken pieces from a mickey of booze and a crescent wrench were lying in the stream.

Events became very confusing after that. As the bus stopped, I began thinking of a way to get out. Avoiding the blood on the floor, then sliding past the people who were now moving into the aisle, was slow going. I was shaking all the way.

Managing to exit the bus soon after the police and ambulance arrived, I placed myself at the edge of the people and vehicles now stopped outside. The police were holding The Rabbit by his arms near the back exit of the bus. They had a lot to say to him. Another police officer was slowly leading the young woman toward a patrol car as a crew wheeled her boyfriend on a gurney toward the ambulance parked near the bus. She wasn't saying anything, but she cast a contemptuous, hate-filled look at him as the gurney slid into the back of the vehicle. My heart did a stutter step when seeing it.

Shakes and nausea began slowly subsiding as I started the long walk home. Thoughts about surprises that could come from rabbits were swimming through my mind as I absent-mindedly brushed small red pieces of glass from the blood spatters on my shirt. A big guy had picked on a little guy and was seriously injured for it, which looked like a form of justice to me. In other words, the big guy had gotten what he deserved, and from a rabbit, of all things. Over the years, my mind would occasionally return to what had happened that afternoon, and the justice I saw in the situation would fade. A big guy picking on a little guy would still be wrong, but I would come to know the damage done to everyone involved by the violence that had happen. And I would come to question why I, and society, so readily accepted violence against males. Such situations became something other than just a good guy-bad guy episode.

What about the young woman? She disappeared when the violence began on the bus. Then, she returned when I saw the virulent look she cast at her companion as he was being loaded into the ambulance. After that, unlike The Rabbit and the young man, she disappeared again. I couldn't remember thinking or talking about her until her sudden return as a vaguely female form while writing this story. In the flashback, she was defined with surprising clarity by the look she had cast at her companion. I still felt the shock that look had caused. The heat I sensed between them as they entered the bus also returned. But her image remained one of mystery accompanied by the impossibility of understanding what was happening to her. She appeared as if she had been violated or abused somehow. Why else would she cast a look of hatred rather than one of shock, worry, compassion, sadness, or any other emotion that was possible?

Being confronted by the mystery of the young woman drove me to create a story about what was happening to her. It began with a memory of another woman who told me about birthing her first and only child. The process eliminated her sense of self-control so profoundly that she never had another child and avoided relationships with men. Instead of being betrayed by a birthing process, the woman on the bus was betrayed by erotic love for the young man. The very libidinous energy that had attracted her to him had produced the abuse of The Rabbit. The violence that occurred that day damaged her as well as the men. She became aware of the trap her love had placed her in and how difficult it would be to escape it. What would she do now? Would her reaction as time passed become as extreme as the other woman's? Or would she chart a more moderate course?

FEEDING TIME IN CAMP

Fire season was upon us, and the weather was very hot and dry. The crew was on early shifts, and the temperature could be more than 100 degrees in the shade by 11 a.m. They were harsh conditions in which to be introduced to my first logging camp. There had been times over the past month or so when it had been hard to see through the sweat-haze. We had already put in six hard hours, and it was a relief to see the push[3] come out waving his wet and dry bulb thermometer to measure the humidity. We could stop work if it was below 40%. After looking at the scale, he waved us toward the crummy. The crew would go to town for four days off since it was our last day of a 10-day shift. I would stay in camp. The prospect of a four-day rest was sweet. There would be time to catch up on personal chores. Recaulking my boots and washing my clothes were long overdue. One could also go swimming off the booms and even use one of the camp boats to go fishing. The cook and pearl diver[4] were staying in too. They were good company and the food would be excellent. Things were looking rosy indeed.

The cook and pearl diver had adopted me, as only two mature women can adopt a young male in the company of older, tougher men. I had come to love and trust them both, as only a young man being fed and looked after can. I still see them standing side by side in the kitchen, forming a perfect square in my memory. The cook had shoulders making the top of the square. In addition to being large, she had rough skin to go with a somewhat gruff and abrasive personality. She was the one that took time off from her cooking to do my disciplining and tough-love episodes. The pearl diver was also quite large, though she didn't strike one as such. She was a gentle soul and had hips that completed the bottom of the square. Her role was to provide solace when life's difficulties struck, wash dishes, and

---

[3] Boss or Superintendent; in this case he owned the camp, too.

[4] Dishwasher.

deliver the excellent food the cook prepared. Their faces and physical shapes showed the changes wrought by the passage of time. They had their dreams over the years, some fulfilled, and some not. They were perfect and wonderful. My memory is filled with pictures of them working together as a team and feeding us in our small world while cleaning up its messes.

I was enjoying a relaxing day reading on my bunk and thinking about going fishing. Every time I glanced up and looked out the door, I saw Coho Salmon breaking the surface of the water in the bay. Then, the cook showed up in the doorway, blocking my view and having a tale to tell.

"There's a bear out there, and it isn't going away," she said.

The situation wasn't outside the realm of possibility, though it was a bit surprising. The camp was in an area with a lot of bears. There were even tales of grizzlies hanging around. But the bears didn't seem to come near the camp, preferring the garbage dump, which was quite a distance away. Camp lore stated grizzlies—brown with a large hump on their back—were much more dangerous than black bears. The latter would usually run if you yelled at them. The other kind would probably run over you. So, quite naturally, my mind fixated on bear colour when I heard one wasn't going away. Portraying a cool and knowledgeable demeanour, while opening wider the crust-laden eyes I had developed in the heat of the past month, I asked: "What colour is it?" Her answer, of course, would determine my direction of travel.

"It's black," she said

With the confidence which comes from receiving a correct answer, I moved lazily to pick my shotgun off its shelf.

After grabbing the two number five Maxim shells I had to go with the gun, and stretching like some hero in a western movie, I asked in my most manly voice, "Where is this bear?"

"It's by the cook shack," she said tightly, maybe even guiltily.

Perhaps I am reading in the guilt here; it's clear I wasn't aware of much at the time. Whatever the case may be, clutching my shotgun, along with my illusions, I said manfully, "Show me."

Let's digress here for some technical bits. They should help with understanding events down the road. Perhaps you can play one of the spaghetti western themes in your head while waiting to find out what happened. It's what I am doing right now, waiting to tell you.

The gun I was carrying was a comparatively simple mechanism. It was a single-shot, Cooey shotgun, a label that immediately tells one that it fires one shot and the spent shell must be replaced by an unfired one to shoot again. The gun had a single barrel supported by a stock made of wood. There was a trigger to fire the gun and a small lever that opened it to allow removal of the spent round and replace it with an unfired one. The procedure to use such a gun also sounds simple. One moved the small lever to open the barrel, remove any spent case, and put a new one in. After replacing the spent shell, you would close the shotgun by lifting the barrel upward, and—Bob's your uncle—the gun would be ready to fire another shot.

Firing the shot wasn't complicated either. The person shooting the gun would hold the stock firmly into his shoulder. Then, after pointing it at the target, he would put his finger on the trigger and squeeze it gently. It all seems simple enough, doesn't it? Nevertheless, there are several other facts you need to know.

Sometimes the old gun I was carrying could screw up by leaving the fired shell stuck in the barrel and make it challenging to remove. Usually, opening the gun after firing it would move the spent case out a bit, but in those instances when it didn't, I had to wiggle the fingernails of my right hand under the rim of the case to remove it. The gun had failed in this regard many times and allowed me much practice in doing this. Such training had made me feel like a bit of a 'dab hand' at reloading, especially after teaching myself to hold a new shell in my left hand to reload while doing the necessary fingernail-wiggling-spent-case-extraction procedure. So, as you can see, there would be some justification for feeling the confidence I did if I was in a fair world. This latter fact leads me to something else you should be aware of.

The statement "two number five Maxim shells" will tell a shooting fan that I would be shooting small lead pellets ideal for hunting pheasants. Such experts might even go on to claim, while enthusiastically providing excruciatingly detailed facts to support their view, that a number five shot is woefully inadequate for hunting bears. The simple truth of the matter is that I don't know why I took the shotgun with me in the first place. Perhaps it was a habit, or I was thinking of firing a shot to scare the bear away.

After the cook and I turned the corner of the bunkhouse, I saw the bear standing near the steps leading up to the kitchen. Observing the correct colour, I loaded my shotgun by putting a shell in the open chamber.

When I was about fifteen feet away from the bear, I yelled, "BUGGER OFF!"

Very macho stuff, you must admit, and perfectly consistent with the music in my head—and possibly yours. It was only when I saw the bear wasn't running but remaining in place looking at me that my macho began to wane. Oddly enough, it seemed to be much closer than fifteen feet around that time, too.

Remaining calm, I decided it was essential to load my shotgun. Looking down, I saw the unfired shell in the chamber from my having already loaded one and immediately became confused. Dire thoughts began flooding my mind, leading to a significant pause in my actions. Meanwhile, the bear just stood there, continuing to observe me.

A gamut of emotions began running through me, beginning with regret for taking a job in the logging camp. There was also a fear engendered by the bear not running on cue, accompanied by a profound desire to return to the simple life I had before going to see it. I didn't want to shoot the bear, just scare it away. Indeed, I had never truly considered that I might have to shoot it. I didn't want to let the cook and pearl diver down, either—what a conundrum.

As for the bear, it looked like it could stand there forever. I had to do something. Since I had only two shells, one would be all that was left if I fired a warning shot. What if it didn't run? What if it got mad at me and charged? OK, how about shooting it, even if I didn't want to?

The deficiencies in my equipment suggested there was too much chance of only wounding it. I hated the idea of killing it but wounding it seemed even worse. And I loathed the idea of being wounded myself. The dilemma was piling upon dilemma.

I'm not sure how long it took me to make up my mind. But, in the end, I decided to fire a warning shot. After all, I had a second shot clenched in my sweaty left fist and had practiced reloading stuck cases.

Closing the shotgun's chamber and mounting it with the stock firmly pulled into my right shoulder, I took the shot while being careful to aim at the ground and not hit the bear. What followed might have been genuinely comical if you were observing from a safe position. An ideal site would be the one the cook and the pearl diver now had. They were both watching through a window from inside the cook shack. In fact, in the middle of the developing situation, I recall being distracted for a moment by seeing them there and wondering how the devil they got to where they were. Their circumstances were entirely different from those for the bear and me. We were together outside in the open air, and I had just fired a shot in its direction.

After I fired the shot, the bear jumped straight up. I can still see it with all four paws off the ground. Then coming down, it began pacing back and forth, growling and shaking its head, obviously upset by the noise. After observing its behaviour with apprehension—budding terror might be more appropriate—I looked down and saw that the spent shell was stuck in the barrel of the shotgun, as I told you could happen before. I would now have to do the fingernail-wiggling procedure to remove the spent case. I was lucky I had practiced because the need for speedy and proficient reloading was quickly becoming excruciatingly important.

Later, I found out the bear's behaviour was similar to 'choice point behaviour' when a rat is learning a maze. I'm sure you can imagine that it has a different effect when an animal armed with large claws and teeth does it while growling and gnashing those teeth, especially when maze walls do not contain it. Luckily, the bear continued its choice point behaviour while I was busy dealing with reloading.

Reloading with a stuck case hadn't proved to be all that difficult before. How easy it is to do when a bear has just been shot at, however, is an entirely different matter. Viewed from a distance, the solution to the problem is still conceptually simple; you worm your fingernails under the rim of the case to get a better purchase, then you pull the spent shell casing out of the gun. Closing the breach firmly after inserting the unfired shell, you would then be at the previously mentioned Bob's-Your-Uncle-ready-to-shoot-again stage.

In keeping with the lore that says any plan requires modification when one tries to carry it out—some say after the first blow falls—I now found worming my fingernails under the case, so the bloody thing—sorry—comes out, to be difficult to do. Of course, one might expect this since any practice I had done wasn't in front of an angry bear. But my thinking hadn't gone that far, and some details were a surprise to me under such new conditions. When starting to reload, the first thing I found was that the opened shotgun had ended up stuck in my right armpit. It should have remained firmly pulled into my shoulder or held down by my right side where access to the open chamber of the gun was easily achieved. I have no idea how the gun got to where it was. Even with a body position resembling a pretzel, the chamber wasn't easy to reach. Not only that, I found my fingernails had become too thick to fit under the rim of the spent case. At this point, I started finding it harder and harder to control the feeling of panic growing in me. Somewhere in all this, you may have begun wondering, as I did, what the bear was doing?

Having taken my eyes off the bear to win the struggle with the stuck case, I still knew he or she (How does one sex a bear?) was still around because of the growling. It was amazing how long the growling lasted with the bear still in approximately the same place. You can bet your last dollar I was listening very carefully for clues its position was changing. I was so aware of these clues that attending to them impeded my performance in doing the spent-case extraction task. Finally, using panic-driven desperation to exert massive force, I succeeded in inserting my nails under the case rim. Frantically pulling the case out of the chamber while only breaking a couple of fingernails, I was ready to reload. The next thing that happened was truly horrifying.

Moving my gaze toward the new shell being held in my left hand while watching my right-hand approach it, I saw the fingers of my left hand slowly open and drop the new shell.

Have you ever experienced one of those silent, slow-motion experiences in life? Your body feels like it almost doesn't exist. Your movements are slow, very slow. There is no sound, except possibly a hissing in the background or some kind of wah-wah sound. You are so tense you have no feeling.

It is like what I experienced while watching the shell travel toward the ground, with my right hand belatedly coming into view chasing it. For some reason, I didn't drop the shotgun at this stage. It was the only thing left to do to complete the way I was screwing up satisfactorily. My right hand did, however, bury its fingers about an inch into the ground when picking up the new shell. Then everything became frenzied as I slammed it, along with the dirt I had picked up into the chamber. Jamming the action closed with a quick jerk of the barrel upwards, I somehow managed to pinch the skin on my right hand in the shotgun's action tearing it. Anyone who has done this wonderful stunt will tell you it really, really hurts. It's certainly worse than breaking a trivial little nail or two.

The river of adrenalin flowing through me in the situation must have suppressed the pain when I tore the skin off. It came later as a reward for my dismal performance. In a state of panic approaching terminal level, I wildly looked up to see what the other member of the comedy show was doing.

Against all the odds and utterly contrary to what I deserved; the bear had decided to leave. Surely it was driven primarily by disgust. Shaking its head while turning to look back every few steps, it kept barking at me and the whole situation. I just stood there watching it dispassionately. Shaking like a leaf, I raised my shotgun with my dirty, bleeding hand and about a pound of dirt in the chamber along with the newly loaded shell—the pound is an exaggeration. Carefully observing the bear moving away while aiming with a profound fatalism, I shot a precisely calculated distance behind it. Showing a satisfying increase in velocity, the bear stopped vocalizing and disappeared rapidly into the bush.

To be honest, at this stage I didn't care if the gun blew up or the bear came back. I was done.

The cook and pearl diver, who, as you already know, observed the whole thing from the safety of the cook shack, came out. They led me by both arms into the kitchen. With tenderness and solicitude, they cleaned and bandaged my injured hand and clipped and smoothed my broken nails while giving me a cup of coffee to keep me occupied. The fact they had fed the bear several times leaked out while we were talking about what had happened.

"He had always gone away before," they carolled in wonderment.

Following this fascinating revelation, they went on to describe how they had never lost confidence in me throughout the whole ordeal. With a warm glow of affection, I heard them suggest I clean my gun in case the bear came back. Fearing they might feed a grizzly next, I quickly pointed out that I had shot my last two shells. It was even the truth.

THE DOG RAN

We were sitting in our chairs in front of the cabin, smoking and talking quietly in the darkness. The man's face was hidden, but I could see it every once in a while, when his cigarette glowed as he took a drag. He could probably see me the same way. There was a warm wind coming up from the river about 50 feet below us, and we were catching it lightly on our faces. The loudness of the rushing water varied with fluctuations in the warm wind, giving the feeling it was approaching and receding. The river was running high for the time of year, and the lights from the village across from us were streaks outlining the currents and rapids. As I looked at their reflections from the water, I began feeling separated from the village and removed from the world around us. The evening was a perfect one for the tale the man told.

Comfortable silences had punctuated our conversation until I asked the man if he ever climbed up to the mountain cave sitting in the face of the mountain across the river. In a place where the Sasquatch was written and talked about, we knew the mountain as a massive darkness in the evening. We knew the cave in its face and the slide it sat above. He told me that he had climbed up to it once and found signs of old fires. Knowing the Spanish had come that far upriver, he called it the Spanish lookout cave. Then the man went quiet, and the quality of his silence changed. Something was on his mind, though I didn't know what it could be.

I don't know how long we sat in silence. As it continued, I began to feel like it was hitting my ears in time with the waxing and waning of the river sounds. My question about the mountain had triggered a memory for him. He must have felt it was important and was wondering how to tell me about it. Whatever was going on inside him, he finally began describing what happened on the mountain. He had taken his dog hunting with him there one day. The dog being part of the story wasn't a surprise. He often took it with him when walking in the bush. But what happened with them on this hike was unusual. It will help you to understand the man's reaction—and mine—if I tell you what he and the dog were like.

He was an honest man with many secrets, if such is possible, and highly intelligent. A sergeant major in the army during WWII. He was also a talented journeyman sheet metal worker for over 45 years. To me, his most remarkable characteristics were his skill working with steel, his fierceness, his awareness of the world around him, and his ability to fight. He fought many times in his life: in smokers during the great depression, on the streets, or in bars. Sparring with Ezzard Charles showed the man his limits. It didn't bother him at all. He just admired Charles for his skill. If it weren't so dark, I would be able to see the scarring across the knuckles of the man's hands. It still strikes me as incongruous that such an intelligent and sensitive person could be so fierce or have such scars, but the truth of it is undeniable. I didn't know until after he died, and a physician told me, that he also had scarring on his brain's frontal and temporal parts. They were due to an injury he suffered as a child. I did know of the event that injured him. I probably knew some sides of him better than anyone else.

The man took me along with him to get the dog. We went onto the reserve to visit an old fellow named Pete. I'm pretty sure Pete was a casualty of WWI, and the First Nations people had taken him in, letting him live on the reserve.

While we were looking at a bunch of puppies in the pen he had built, Pete asked me which one I wanted. No doubt it was a put-up job by the adults. But I didn't know that, and after looking at the squirming ball of them, as well as picking each of them up, I chose one. Seeing my decision, Pete asked if we wanted the tail cut short. Hearing that we did, he picked up the puppy. Putting its tail in his mouth, he felt around with his teeth, then bit the tail off. Seeing my fear after spitting it out, he described how he was feeling the cartilage with his teeth to find a joint in the tail. Biting the tail off that way, he said, ensured that the stub wouldn't be sensitive on its end and didn't hurt the pup as much as doing it any other way. Pete told us he had left the stub long enough so the pup would be able to tuck it when he grew up. (Pete was right. The pup hardly yelped when the tail came off. The stub wasn't sensitive when the dog grew up, and it could tuck its tail under exceptional circumstances, as you will see.)

Encouraged by our rapt attention, Pete went on to tell us that the dogs were a Husky/Airedale cross, scared of water, and basically nothing else on the planet. He said Airedales were trained as bear dogs by getting ten or twelve of them together and putting them on a bear. The seven or eight who lived would then be smart enough not to be killed and be great bear dogs.

I never saw a bear used for training purposes and had reservations about chasing animals with dogs, so you'll have to decide for yourself how true the story was. Pete was right about the dog's characteristics, though. It didn't like swimming but proved its courage and fierceness on many occasions. We had come to rely on its superior ability to detect things, give warnings, and fight. Indeed, we believed all of these things to be the very basis of the ancient relationship between dogs and humans.

The long tail stub proved to be significant, too. The dog tucked it on the rare occasion it was in trouble with the man. But it didn't do so around bears or other dogs. It was curious about cougar sign, and the man told me he saw it chase one once. All-in-all, it was an excellent companion and an important one to go into the bush with, especially on the hunt he was telling me about that evening we sat above the river.

After hiking on the mountain for a couple of hours, the man and the dog emerged from the heavy woods only to find his memory had played a trick on him. They had come out at the slide rather than the country on the other side of it where they were going to hunt. Now, the only choices were to cross the slide or backtrack and find a way below it. Finding neither option to be particularly attractive, he decided to go across. It was dangerous, like any slide, but it was an old one, and it looked stable enough. Finding a stick to balance with, he and the dog started across. They were nearly a third of the way when the rocks underneath him began moving. Losing his balance, he fell, dropping his rifle. Continuing to hold himself in place with the stick while fearfully hoping the whole slide would not start moving, he watched his rifle go over a precipice below him. I could feel the increase in his fear as he re-lived that moment. He hadn't been aware there was a precipice below him. After a period of silence, the man described how he recovered his balance and slowly walked back off the slide. The dog, which had preceded him, had turned and jumped over him on its way back as the slide began moving.

The man told me that if the dog had continued across, he might have done so himself. Reflecting on the difference that would have made, he went on to say he wasn't sure whether he intended to continue the hunt. He just didn't want to leave the rifle. So, after sitting together for a while looking back at the slide, he and the dog began making their way down into the country below. After somewhat of a hike, they found a small canyon hidden near the bottom of the slide.

This is close to what he told me: "The canyon stretched across the base of the slide. It was narrow and felt unnatural, like a weight slowly pushing against you. There wasn't much light in there. The evergreens on its side blocked it, and the place was cold, even though the day was warm. Some of the tree branches had moss hanging from them that was slightly moving in air currents."

By now, I was waiting for the pause that followed, as well as the drag on his cigarette. For some reason, I had a feeling of being in the presence of something old while I was listening to him talk. It was a strange feeling. I didn't know if it was coming from me or him. The tinge of fear in his voice made me feel tense. It magnified the feeling of removal that had been growing in me that evening. Feeling removed and in the presence of age, while wondering what would come next, I took a drag on my own cigarette with my eyes riveted on the glow from his.

Believing that the rifle would be somewhere in the canyon, he started into it with the dog beside him. Fear began growing in him almost immediately, and the dog remained close to his leg. He felt his pace slowing as if he was walking against the resistance. Finally, seeing his rifle lying at the bottom of the precipice, he wasn't relieved. His fear remained, and he stopped with his gaze locked on it. Not wanting to leave the rifle, he began willing himself to walk over and pick it up. Suddenly, the dog, which had continued walking beside him, raised its hackles, tucked its stub, and ran back the way they had come without a sound. The reaction of the dog terrified him. He said the hair on the back of his neck went straight up.

The situation came close to defeating the man. He felt safety was in the direction the dog had run. But all he could think of was how he should not turn his back to the scene in front of him to go there. Not seeing any reason for his, or the dog's, fear, he stood unmoving on the edge of panic. Still not wanting to leave his rifle, however, he eventually began forcing himself to move forward. His legs and body were stiff with fear, but somehow, he managed to keep moving. Still believing any quick movement might start something dangerous after reaching his rifle, he slowly moved his hand toward the gun then picked it up. He then began slowly backing up in the direction the dog had run without turning. When he finally turned around, he didn't run but continued walking slowly while watching his backtrail. He would typically look back to keep his backtrail familiar. An unfamiliar backtrail could confuse a person who was losing their way and even lead to panic. On this occasion, however, he was looking back because he was afraid something might be following him, not because he was becoming lost.

We sat there for a long time in silence, digesting his story and reflecting on the fear exhibited by the dog. The courage it had shown throughout its life made it hard for either of us to imagine what had caused it to run. Eventually, just having to know, I asked him what he thought was in the valley.

Continuing to sit there silently thinking while I waited, he took in a deep breath, followed by a deep sigh, and quietly said: "There was something there, but I don't know what it was."

We continued sitting there alone with our thoughts, at peace with each other.

The man and I saw each other occasionally after he told the story, but I don't recall us talking about it after that night on the river. Mentioning the Sasquatch at the beginning of telling his story wasn't an accident. Having spent time in that country during my formative years, I was aware of mythical creatures existing in the wilderness. The Sasquatch was the one that was supposed to be living there. It was only natural that I had thought of its presence as the story unfolded. But, when I asked the man what was in the valley, he didn't mention the Sasquatch, though he certainly knew what it was. He simply said something was there, leaving me with a question.

The man passed on. I had seen him the night before he died. We laughed and smoked a cigar. I told him I cared about him while he sat there in his wheelchair smoking—love was a difficult word for me at that time. The following day, he was gone, and a hole opened in me, though I didn't cry. His ashes were stored away. I wished him well on his journey and, as the man would say, ending his, ". . . and we move on."

THE RAPTOR CAME BACK

The man left two problems when he died, though I was unaware of them at the time. One problem was that I didn't put him properly to rest. The other came from the powerful story he told about his unexplainable experience. He didn't say Sasquatch, but how he told his story implied a mythical creature was present during the hunt he and his dog were on. And the Sasquatch was the mythical one that was supposed to be living in the country we were in. What I knew of the man suggested that his thoughtful look while only saying something was there, rather than naming it, was done on purpose. I could only guess, of course. But when he told me the story, I saw no use for fantasy and myth besides entertainment. The man either knew they were important and decided to leave me a clue instead of telling me outright. Or, he didn't know and was thinking about it. He had left me with questions to be answered, either way. My answer for putting him to rest and finding a use for myth began when I went on my first hunt in the north years after his death. Hunting was something the man had taught me to do from a young age.

My hunting partner and I had landed on a runway made during WWII about 100 kilometres, as the crow flies, off the Alaska Highway. The runway was in a valley near the head of a river. It was pitted and cracked in places, with small bushes growing over its surface, but light airplanes could still use it. The conifers, which grew on the surrounding mountains, looked smaller than those further south, and the amount of bare mountain above the treeline was larger. The deep pathways in the valley had all been made by wild animals. In my late 40s, much of my time was spent in places that weren't wild. The feeling of being isolated from them flooded into me as the plane that had dropped us flew away.

It was late afternoon when we landed, and one wasn't supposed to hunt for many hours upon arrival. So, deciding to hold off on hunting until the following morning, we explored instead. It was dark when we were returning to camp along the old runway. One could barely make out the little bushes close to us as we went from clear space to clear space between them. Then, out of the corner of my eye, I saw my partner begin to wheel around. Following him, I saw a huge, black shape passing behind us. It was very close and completely silent. We were now entirely immersed in the wild as we stood silently watching. Arriving back in camp later we both acknowledged the presence of that dark silent form and even laughed while guessing it had been a moose. Our soft laughter was mildly ironic. We had been moved by what we saw. The silent shadow passing us added to the altered state we were in. It would stay with us throughout a challenging hunt.

The pilot had told us that he would check on us in three or four days. Laying out a tarp would signal that we had game or some other kind of problem. He would then land. After day three without a flyby, we suspected something might be wrong. On day four, an eagle held position over us in air currents. It was the first time we had seen one there. Seeing the raptor somehow confirmed the fear that had been developing in me that something was wrong and that the pilot wasn't coming back. (Immersion in the wilderness can make one sensitive to such signs.) Later, we learned that he had crashed and died while checking out a potential drop site on the side of a mountain after leaving us. I became depressed. (This was not an unusual reaction. There were a number of us the pilot had dropped in other parts of the country, and some of them, especially those who were alone, even reported becoming suicidal when they realized something was wrong.)

Fly-casting to overcome feeling depressed—the creek didn't have any trout—I remember thinking it might take us a few days, but we could walk to the Alaska highway. We had suitable clothing; four pounds of lentils and the rest of our food; an elk down; and water in the creek. So, we were well-supplied, in good shape, and wouldn't starve or die of thirst on our way out. We might lose the rest of the elk, but mother nature, with her pragmatic approach, would recycle it. The thoughts didn't take long to occur, and the depression went with them as they passed through. With faith that our problem could be resolved, my partner and I decided to stay. There was, however, another factor coming into play.

The day we were dropped onto the airstrip was pleasant and sunny. But over the four days it took us to realize there was something amiss, the weather had been changing in a way that would begin breaking us down. Temperatures would hover in the low forties (Fahrenheit), and squalls with a cold wind, driven rain, and sleet started coming off the divide—perfect hypothermia weather. It is hard to believe how relentless these conditions turned out to be. There were brief sunny periods over the time we were there, but they weren't warm enough and didn't last long enough for us to get dry. Soon, our boots, spare socks, and underwear were damp in the morning. We had no relief when we woke up chilled by the dampness and low temperatures. It became harder and harder for our bodies to warm up. Lying awake at night in our tent, my companion and I listened for the wind that would come off the divide. We would brace ourselves when he heard it roaring toward us through the forested slopes, sounding like a vast, relentless flood or freight train. As the wind hit, the tent would shake with unspeakable violence. We truly felt it was a miracle that it didn't fly away.

One day, a German fellow arrived at our camp during a brief sunny period. He was alone and had been walking for several days. Believing he could live off the land, all he carried was a sleeping bag in his pack, a bow, a sheath knife, a canteen, and very little food. By the time he reached us, he hadn't found any food and was very hungry and cold. Our traveler seemed unmoved by his difficulty finding food, but he was grateful for being fed. He was also friendly and considerate, signalling our camp while still a distance away. When asked, he told us that he was heading across the divide to a fort or trading post on the other side. He wasn't concerned when we told him of the rainstorms and strong winds that had been coming off the divide. Temperatures in the low forties didn't worry him, nor did the fact we couldn't tell him what he would find when he arrived at the post he was heading for. As we talked, it became apparent that he was very conversant with the thinking and activities of our First Nations people, whose workshops he had attended in Germany. (Later, I was able to ask a sun dancer about the workshops. He confirmed the interest he found in Germany while visiting there, going on to say he believed some Germans knew more about first nation's culture than he did. We both smiled. After some time passed, I even had a rueful laugh about what he had said. It would be difficult for me to explain my own culture to Germans, or anyone else.) Listening to our visitor describe the workshops he had participated in, I had the strangest feeling that he had lost something and was now looking for it. It made me think of Germany's loss of the father during WWII. After feeding our guest and letting him warm up at our fire, we gave him some of our supplies—my partner, who had planned the food, had built-in some surplus. Telling him of a grizzly kill that would be near his path, we then watched him head on his way toward the divide. My partner was concerned about the fellow. Being an experienced woodsman, who had run outward bound programs, he felt the man was foolish. My feelings were different, though I did wonder if he would survive. I began carrying a picture of human bones in my head. They rested among the frost-covered rocks on the divide while being polished by the cold winds laden with sleet and snow blowing there. But, to me, it seemed that our visitor would accept dying on his journey, and it was a place where he would be willing to rest.

At the 11-day mark—one day after we were to be picked up—a plane landed on the airstrip. The man who would fly us out described what had happened to our other pilot. We had liked the young pilot, and we were distressed by what had happened to him. But, by this time, we were tired and anxious to begin moving toward home. We didn't say much, except that we were sorry. We didn't mention that we weren't surprised by what had happened. Later, I came to feel the tragedy of the young pilot's death. It wasn't enough to make his loss acceptable, but those at the funeral said he had died while doing what he loved to do.

Our 1000-kilometre drive toward our home was contemplative and quiet as the altered state present during our hunt began slowly receding. The meat my partner had shot had been saved. We were now passing beautiful scenery, and the weather was outside our vehicle's windows. We rented a motel for one night when we were closer to civilization to allow ourselves some recovery time as well as a meal we hadn't had to cook ourselves. Somewhere in the altered state that existed during our hunt, though I'm not sure exactly when, I told my hunting partner the story about the hunt the man and the dog had been on. The logical time would have been soon after seeing that shadow passing behind us.

My companion knew about mythical creatures that arose in the wilderness and didn't deny his feelings about them or the mystery surrounding them. His opinion concerning them was similar to my own. We could joke about the creatures, and he even coined the expression the *great googly woogly* to describe their presence, changing my vocabulary forever. We both found feeling their presence to be helpful and relied on it to tell us something might be around. My friend also believed that he could explain what the man experienced that day in the hidden canyon. His view was that the man's experience came from being in a place cats passed through. Later, he took me on a hike into a valley where he had felt the same things the man had described—darned if he wasn't right, too. There was cat sign there. I could feel a chill and became increasingly uneasy while we were in there, which I mentioned, but little else was said.

Perhaps my friend's explanation was correct? It was indeed a compelling one and one that provided the comfort of the tangible. The fact the dog had silently run, however, and had once chased a cougar, caused me to wonder. The next stage in what was becoming my own personal Chautauqua came when we were on a hunt even further north.

We were hunting for moose on the Tetsa River. It was a new country for us. We could see the usual mountains with conifers on them, along with the considerable distance the mountains travelled above the timberline. The broad stretches of river rock leading out to the low water showed us how high the river could run at other times of the year. Unlike the previous hunt, the weather was temperate and would remain that way. We expected moose would come down off the hills to drink. So, we separated, with my partner going up the river and me going down. We planned to meet back at camp around noon.

By around 10 o'clock, I hadn't seen anything but a large beaver. It was swimming in a slough beside the trail I was following. The beaver's head was big enough that, from a distance, it looked like it might be a bear, which provided some excitement. But after a few minutes of observing it with my binoculars, I was forced to acknowledge it was a large beaver. Boredom began setting in as the chance of having a successful hunt diminished. The heat from the sun was also making me sleepy. I was at the point where I could identify numerous reasons why it would be better not to get a moose when I saw a big log laying high and dry on the rocks about twenty feet from the bank of the river. It looked comfortable to lie on. Running water had smoothed the log's surface, and there was an excellent gradual dish in its middle. Overcome by drowsiness, I walked out, laid in the dish, put my rifle across my chest, and fell asleep in the sunshine. Who knows how long I slept before suddenly becoming fully awake? Remaining very still, while wondering if a bear was nearby, I slowly looked around, but there was nothing to see. Still feeling strange while walking over to the riverbank, I noticed a speck over a distant mountain that appeared to be moving toward me. As the dot got closer, it turned into a raptor and a good-sized one at that.

When the raptor reached where I was, it began dropping down and circling rather than passing by. Continuing to circle, the bird started screaming while dropping lower and lower. It even tilted its head to look directly at me. Feeling singled out, aggressive, and afraid because of that direct look, I recall thinking that I might have to poke it in the bum with the barrel of my rifle if it came any lower.

Emitting a final scream, the raptor flew back in the direction from which it had come. Watching it become a speck in the sky again, I was surprised to see it begin to get bigger. The raptor was coming back. My feelings changed from aggressiveness to puzzlement. What was going on? Was there something around I didn't know about? When it arrived, the raptor did the very same thing it had done before. If anything, the session felt longer and even more intense. After it left for the second time to become a speck, I stood there waiting for it to come back. But the speck disappeared, and the raptor was gone. The bird's behaviour was bizarre. It had singled me out. Not only that, it had come a long way to do it and did so twice. It was beyond my understanding. I couldn't see or smell a kill near me, nor was a baby raptor around or even another predator. The place was quiet in all respects, adding to the impact of what had gone on.

Arriving back in camp, I saw my partner putting the coffee pot on the fire. He reported having the same lack of hunting success that I had. When I told him about falling asleep on the log, and the experiences that followed with the raptor, however, both of us happily entered the domain of myth and mystery—the home of the great googly woogly. Neither of us was particularly fey, but we both found the raptor's behaviour to be fascinating and began trying to figure out what the events might mean.

Becoming increasingly puzzled by our task, we thought of looking for a shaman with knowledge of local myths to help us. Then I remembered the ashes of the man who told me the story that night on the river. Recalling his fierceness and the fierceness of the raptor, I began thinking the message might concern him. After telling my friend about the man's ashes and how they hadn't been scattered, he suggested it was time to move them on. The best way to do so would be to put them in the river we had been sitting above when he told his story. After a pause to think about the issue, we settled back in satisfaction.

A family member helped me move the man's belongings. The water system had to be repaired, and his house and shop cleared out. The house had been unoccupied for a long time, and the property was being sold. I had started feeling removed from it when we were coming across the river to do the job. I knew that I no longer belonged but would carry memories from there. Completing the repairs in a single day, we began loading the boat. Some of the man's possessions had disappeared, undoubtedly used in other places. Enough remained, however, to easily fill our boat and leave some things for those coming behind us. The load we stacked in the boat was top-heavy and awkward. Fatigue and the fact we were losing light contributed to the poor job we did of loading.

Intending to scatter the man's ashes as we returned across the river, and wanting them to travel downstream rather than into shallows where they would settle out, I tried to hold the boat in the middle of the river. My action, combined with the awkwardness of the load, put us into a side-to-side feedback loop that kept threatening to spill us into the water. I could barely control the erratic motion, causing the ashes to be poured into the water in a clump rather than a neat steady stream. I saw them rapidly floating away and felt the tears that had been waiting come into my eyes. The man and the presence that came with his story were leaving on their way north. Now, feeling my loss, I recalled how he had cared for me throughout all my years. The feelings I had were brief. They broke through the struggle I was having with the boat.

I can feel the loss as I sit here now, though time and acceptance have made it less painful. Placing the man's ashes in the river was the conclusion of my part in his story. It seems entirely fitting that it ended during a struggle.

At times, I see the man and the dog in my mind. He is flying over the wilderness up north, fierce and free. He is watching the dog run free and unafraid below. I watch until they are only dots going away from me toward the distant mountains. There is an ache in my heart, and my eyes begin to fill while watching them. I am happy they are there.

Logging
vs
Sociology

Terry McGarvey, illustration credit

JONESY'S GYPPO

The *Beaver* turned to land and approach the stiff leg at Jonesy's logging camp and tie up. The glimpse I had as it was tilting in its turn was brief, but it was long enough to look down and see that the camp I was heading for was probably a 'gyppo.' The word gyppo could mean many things. To those of us on the west coast of British Columbia, it implied logging in rugged country, a small-sized operation, a hardscrabble existence, and using equipment that was not the best. In the late 1950s and early 1960s, gyppos usually got tough wood. Out-and-out dishonesty was rare, but some bending of rules could happen. They paid higher wages because it was necessary to get and hold their men. The prominent union outfits had more amenities, most of the wood, and set the standards for working conditions. I had begun my logging travels about three years before in a camp that looked to be almost twice as large as Jonesy's. The clerk at an agency had told me that I would have to fill in rather than naming a job I would be doing while at the camp. So, I was a little unsettled and wondered what Jonesy would be like and what my job would be during the flight.

After working with him for several months, I would be able to tell you that Jonesy, in contrast to his camp, was very large. He was even bigger than life in some ways, coming in at a very loud six foot three inches and 275 pounds. Contrary to the opinion of some, big athletic guys tend to be bright. In any terms that matter, a man must be running a gyppo and surviving as Jonesy had. He was the only guy who ever fired me, too. I didn't have the heart to defend myself at the time. When I went back to the agency to sign out again, however, I was told that the daft giant asked them to send me back. What do you do with a guy like that? It was part of the spirit of the man that he could admit to making a mistake. But the camp had soured for me, and it was time for me to leave. I wasn't there when his end came in a collision between him, his Cadillac, and a bridge abutment. It would have taken at least that much to put him down. They said he had been drinking in a bar, too, which seems probable. A bit of the shine, some might say glare, went out of the world when that fateful collision happened.

Jonesy was in the small cookshack doing paperwork when I arrived. My memories of that first meeting are sketchy. He must have confirmed who I was, and he would have told me where to bunk. He also invited me to make up a fourth in a game of kitchen bridge that evening with him and his other two captives, though he didn't put it quite that way. The latter were a man and wife team who lived in a trailer separate from the rest of us. The man was one of the camp's machine operators and proved to be a good one. His wife was the cook, and she was good at her job too. They were hard-working, quiet people. I never got to know either of them very well, but our experience together that night was memorable.

The Bridge Game

When playing bridge in the same game as Jonesy, the first thing one noticed was that he walked a fine line in his relentless commitment to winning. His will, in this regard, was as large as his massive body. One felt there was no limit to the lengths he would go to inspire you to make, or not make, a mistake. He did not discriminate in this. You felt the threat whether you were his partner or a member of the enemy team. In critical situations, he would lean toward you, impaling you with the bulging eyes in his enormous head, and do everything but reach across and grab the wrong card, or the right one, out of your hand. It was my turn to come under his gentle regard while I was deciding to make the play that would lead to one of his finer moments.

We were playing the last rubber in a close game, with the contract resting on how I played trumps. There were only two trumps in Jonesy and his partner's hands, the king and a small one. Holding the ace and queen of trumps, I was facing the question of whether to finesse. On Jonesy's mind was the fact that he had the two outstanding trumps and was sitting on my right. The situation was fraught with peril for his team. If I played the queen after leading through him, finessed in other words, his king would fall under my ace on my next play, and his team would lose. I suspect his entire life had become compressed into contemplating that dreadful moment in which his king would fall.

He was watching me so intently and willing me to make the wrong decision so strongly that I felt like a lamb in the presence of a lion. (I understand some warriors can voluntarily withdraw their testicles into their bodies to protect themselves when attacked. It is a lesser-known fact that a lamb can also do it, albeit involuntarily. Take my word for it.) I felt a profound sense of finality even that day, watching my trembling hand reach over to the dummy to play a small trump. The lion had already slapped down a card hard enough to dent the surface of the table while I was on my way over—not the king... a small trump... out of turn, too... he's still staring at me... Is he bluffing? With a misplaced sense of pride, I must tell you the lamb had conceived a plan despite being under duress. It would lead through Jonesy while watching him closely. If he didn't play the king, I would rise with the ace playing for the drop of the king from the victim on the left. Having read a book once and probably gotten it wrong, it was my version of the principle of restricted choice. It grieves me to tell you that the 'lamb' tried to follow my doomed but brilliant strategy, even though any idiot would guess Jonesy held the errant king just by looking at him. However, the careful analysis I intended to do had become lost in the shock caused by his aggressively playing out of turn. Reflexively, I grabbed a card from my hand and played it. Looking back, I believe I was lucky it was even a trump, let alone unlucky because it was the ace.

Sadly, regardless of how sincere one is, how potentially brilliant, or how hard they are trying in the face of adversity, the punishment for being wrong in such circumstances can be immediate and profound. Life is hard in this respect, as John Wayne noted. May he rest in peace. But it is even harder if one is stupid, as he also noted.

Those of us at that bridge table entered a brief period of stunned silence when I played the ace instead of the queen. Jonesy, unrepentant for playing out of turn and knowing all along the right play for me to make, paused too. By this time, I knew that any pause was unusual for him. He was reputed to react instantly, like a ravening hyena smelling blood. However, on this occasion, he appeared stunned into a temporary state of immobility by my act. It was an unexpected error and so entirely at variance with what he believed "HE" would do that he could not conceive of anyone doing it. My heart plummeted with the realization that the lamb part of me was wrong.

Seeing the sun begin to shine on his entire life, Jonesy exploded out of his chair. Continuing to play out of sequence, while slapping down his king, which was now unbeatable, he let out a roar loud enough to stop shipping three islands over. His jubilation at winning was profound. Continuing to roar, he began slamming his huge feet on the floor with every ounce of his 275 pounds. While Jonesy was jumping in ecstasy, however, another force was at play. It allowed him a few jumps to enjoy himself, then suddenly opened the floor and let him go through. It took us a few moments to raise our heads and look when the jumping and roaring abruptly stopped. When we finally did peek, we saw the top of Jonesy's head protruding just above the edge of the table. I recall having an errant thought, as one can have in such moments, that he may well have gone down far enough to hit his testicles on the floor. I hoped he had enough time to retract them on the way down.

After a moment of profound shock, Jonesy began shouting for us to help him get out. All I can remember from this point on is feeling terror and confusion on my way to the nearest exit. To this day, I do not know how he escaped from the fix he was in. It must have taken quite an effort. To indicate the largeness of the man's spirit, however, he showed no signs of harbouring a grudge concerning my strategic retreat. Maybe winning the rubber was enough for him. As for me, there was always pain to accompany the ecstasy and humour in most situations in his camp. Whatever one might say about him, Jonesy was a man of 'ideas' with a rough sense of humour and a strong will to follow through on things.

Job Assignment

After finding out about my inability to play in his bridge game, Jonesy still faced the question of which job to assign me. He attacked this problem outside the cookshack the following day. However, instead of telling me where to go and what to do, he interviewed me. His interview was thorough and took some adjusting to on my part. But, always willing to talk about logging and myself, I soon entered the flow and described my logging experience. I have included some of the vocabulary we used to increase interest and save the colour that existed in logging at that time. Knowing about things we did on the job and how we talked about them should help you appreciate future events. It may even help to prevent losing valuable language. I understand the industry has changed quite a bit since then. It will be up to you to decide whether the changes have been for the better. Or whether, as I suspect, the romance in the enterprise has pretty much disappeared.

As Jonesy surmised, I had been logging in a few camps before arriving in his and had experienced various activities. Consequently, he likely felt I could do most jobs suitable for a 'riggin-rat.' The term isn't necessarily insulting. It indicates someone who generally labours with various types of implements and equipment used in logging, but doesn't do more elevated things like being an overall boss, running machines, felling trees, and so on. Much of my experience, though not all, involved putting chokers on logs (setting chokers) or unhooking them from logs (chasing) in one situation or another. (A choker is a kind of lasso made from cable. One end of the lasso is put around a log and holds it while the other end is attached to something that can pull it somewhere. Think of cowboys roping cattle without the horse and using cable instead of a rope. Chokermen, not cowboy, was the name for those who put chokers on the logs, and those taking them off were called chasers.) Ultimately the end goal of it all was to get the logs to a mill somewhere. Nowadays, I understand that setting chokers may not even be necessary. One can simply drive a machine up to a tree, cut it down, pick it up, put it on a truck, then take it to a mill. It must be more efficient and certainly less labour-intensive. But it does sound a bit less romantic, as I have implied.

During his interview, Jonesy appeared to accept my experience as a whistle punk.[5] He acknowledged my experience as chokerman

---

[5] A whistle punk carried a long coil of wire with a switch on the end, and tooted signals when he, or she, received the order from those in authority. There were many signals for many purposes, and the person doing the punking had to know them all. I suspect whistle punks went the way of the great auk, with the invention of a battery-

and chaser as something to be expected, but my stint as riggin slinger received a slight raising of eyebrows. It was a job with more responsibilities.

Jonesy also noticed that I had worked at man-and-a-half jobs with various equipment. My failings were legion, but one could not say I was a lazy worker. Nor did I disrespect money; such jobs usually paid more. I just put money second in importance to logging. Sometimes I think I would have done it just for the fun of it all.

During my interview, Jonesy didn't show any substantial interest until he heard I had done a stint as a third boom man pimping on a grapple. It was the "pimping on a grapple" that got him, probably for different reasons than just about any other person in the world but a logger would have. It was likely why he decided to put me "chasing second loading on a heel boom." I felt the assignment was worrisome.

Pimping on a grapple meant helping load logs on a truck. The job entailed such things as; positioning the logging truck in the landing when it showed up to get the logs; helping unload the trailer and attaching it to the logging truck; connecting the airlines, and building up the air for the brakes. (It might help in appreciating the romance of all this, if you know that I held and guided the towing shaft of the trailer, after the grapple lifted it off the truck. As the engineer swung the trailer, I guided the shaft until it made connection with the truck by means of a 'bull prick' located on the shaft's end. Who says loggers or truckers do not have an imagination?) Once the trailer was secured, the grapple, which had a big set of pincers that gripped, lifted, and released the logs while loading them on the truck, went into action.

Gaily running back and forth as the loading was being done, I stamped the ends of each log with a hammer, which had numbers and letters on its head to identify the claim the logs had come from. It was loads of fun making sure to hit the logs before they hit me. After the truck left the landing with a full load, I would go back to fulfilling my role as third boom man, something even further removed from what Jonesy intended me to do.

Combined with pimping on a grapple, third boom man was an excellent job for a young chap like me, though it had little to do

---

operated, talky- tooter that hung on a riggin slingers belt. We didn't even call it WiFi back then.

with a second loader, heel boom, or tongs. There were many logging stories to listen to from the head boom man and many cognitive and physical skills to learn. I broke (took apart) jackpots on a lake with my trusty pike pole and cork boots. (Jackpots were piles of logs lying all over each other that resulted from being dropped into the lake. The piles could range from only two logs to lord knows how many.)

Not only was the action during the job fun, but it also provided numerous opportunities to fall into the lake during hot weather—be sure to leave your pack of cigarettes on the raft before the accident. After the jackpots were all broken apart, I would buck logs to appropriate lengths using a big power saw mounted on a raft. Then, bucking finished, I was usually sent to do other things like help the head boom man fill the sweep, which positioned the logs to be picked up by the grapple. Or, he would get me to bore holes in logs to make them into boomsticks. There was always something going on, and time went fast. I had good memories of the job while talking to Jonesy, though I suspect part of my enthusiasm came from not doing it long enough to fall into the lake in the winter.

A critical point for me during the job assignment interview, however, was that my previous activities didn't seem likely to have prepared me to do what Jonesy wanted me to. The only tongs I had seen, up until working for him, were for picking up sugar cubes for tea, not for loading logs onto a logging truck–I supposed this is what that clerk at the hiring agency was talking about when he told me I would have to fill in somewhere. When I mentioned my concern to Jonesy, he said he thought I would learn fast and do okay.

Chasing Second Loading:

Looking at the job site that first morning, I saw a loading machine, a heel boom, a spar tree, a skyline, a pile of logs, and a logging truck. The spar tree was large, though not exceptionally high as such trees went. It had been limbed, topped at about 90 feet, and left standing. The heel boom, which was a bunch of logs connected side-by-side, hung horizontally from the spar tree. Cables attached to each side of the boom allowed the loading machine to pull it in an arc around the tree. The arc was large enough to position it over the pile of logs in the landing and then move them to the logging truck for loading. A cable ran down the middle of the boom, which went through a block at its end. (A block is a pulley with a large gooseneck on it that allows it to be held in place. There were many types of blocks of various sizes, shapes, and weights used in logging. Typically, they were heavily constructed and very strong.) The cable running through the block connected to the handles of a set of tongs. The tongs (Tongs is a tricky singular. There was only one tong. The plural just sounds better to my ear.), which I was looking at with considerable interest, were hanging above the pile of logs. They looked to weigh about 90 pounds and resembled a big, heavy set of deformed steel scissors rather than the dainty sugar tongs I had seen.[6] The arms of the scissors, to continue the analogy, hung with their ends pointing toward the ground. They curved to fit around a log and had hooks at their ends that pointed back to prevent it from falling out when they picked it up. Like scissors, a steel pin connected the arms while still allowing them to open and close. Strong steel handles at the top of the arms, to which the loading line connected, completed the assembly. The tongs I was looking at with such interest were hanging immobile in the quietly moving morning air.

The operation of the system proved to be straightforward and effective. When the tongs were set on a log, the engineer running the loading machine pulled on the loading line, which closed the tongs, allowing them to hold the log. Continuing the pull on the loading line lifted the log, and it indexed (heeled) into the boom. Once it was high enough to clear the stakes on the logging truck, the engineer pulled the boom in an arc using the previously mentioned cables connected to its sides. He positioned the log over the truck and lowered it by slackening the loading line while allowing enough slack to remove the tongs. This kind of heel boom setup was becoming old style, and I doubt you would find many like it today. The industry was in transition, and many other camps had grapples. Old style or not, the system worked well. It was the crew that mattered in making

---

[6] My weight estimate was close. These probably came from the Queen Charlotte Islands, now called Haida Gwai. The timber we were dealing with was big, but there was huge timber up there.

it run. Jonesy's team, which included a head loader, and a loading engineer, in addition to me as a prospective second loader, turned out to be a good one.

The head loader impressed me as a decent sort and an excellent loader. He had a comprehensive knowledge of logging and supervised all aspects of the general running of the landing. If such weren't obvious, he selected the logs for loading, determined where they were placed on the truck, and showed me how to set tongs, all in jig time. My efforts soon melded with his and the engineer. The latter was also a decent man and very good at his job. He was smooth in handling the loading machine, which was priceless on this job. He brought me along gradually with his faultless handling of the loading line. There were any number of ways he could have screwed with me, but he never did. When we left camp one time, I found out that he was an admitted alcoholic and helpless when he drank. It came as a shock, as he never drank in camp. I believe being in camp was his way of staying alive. He wasn't the first guy I had seen who was this way, but he was the first I had to carry home on one trip out.

My job as a second loader was to put (set) the tongs on the logs. When you set tongs, the engineer running the loading machine swings them toward you by moving the boom over the pile of logs. You move to the tongs and grab them on their way by. Holding one tong arm at its end with one hand and the cable connected to the tong handles with the other, you carry the tongs to the log you have chosen. You then throw the free tong arm over the side of the log furthest from you and drop the tong arm you are holding down the side closest to you on the way by. Continuing to move, you then go to a safe place. As you might surmise, the engineer is feeding slack throughout the process. (You can imagine how important it is for him to do his part well.) After you set the tongs, he begins lifting the log. While he is doing all this, of course, you are watching from a safe position and getting ready for the next turn. It was an exciting job, and it was fun. I even learned how the head loader selected logs to load a logging truck. We turned out to be a good crew, and we were soon off to the races. We loaded tons of wood. The angels sang, and the tongs felt light. Even the weather was good.

Jonesy must have become curious while counting the truckloads of logs arriving six or seven miles away in his camp. He turned up one day to watch us load and, presumably, to see why things were going so well. (Logs hitting the water meant we'd all get paid.) For the longest time, Jonesy just stood there watching us operate. I could feel his gaze regarding me as I set tongs. It was not the same stare that he used in the bridge game. He did not look negative as much as puzzled. Since I was new on the job, watching me was only to be expected. Nevertheless, I started becoming a bit nervous as he continued to stand there. What in the hell was he looking at, anyway?

Finally, coming to some decision, he leaped onto the pile, saying: "Watch."

The engineer swung the tongs to him and, using only one hand, Jonesy grabbed the tongs at one end and threw it onto a log. Continuing to direct glances at me all the while, he set a few more tongs this way. Then, jumping off the pile with beads of sweat on his forehead and a big grin on his homely mug, he stood there watching to see what I would do.

The guy outweighed me by 100 pounds.

How does one say it politely: 'My testicles were on the line?'

With a profound feeling of fatalism, reminiscent of the bridge game, I jumped up on the pile to set tongs using one hand. The engineer was helping me all the way—he was that good—and, somehow, I managed to do a turn. My performance was certainly not as graceful as Jonesy's, but it was still a success, after a fashion.

Jonesy just stood there looking at me with my heaving chest and said: "Needs work."

I had stood tall, but then I started bleating about how I had to set tongs all day. I cringe at the memory. Will I never learn to leave well enough alone? Jonesy, an expert at handling men, especially gullible young ones, sauntered away, satisfied with the effect he had.

We never did it while he was around, but the head loader, the engineer, and I practiced one-handed loading when a good log came up. It was a team effort, and we became good at it, but mostly I continued using two hands. Besides improving my one-handed loading, I also felt that interspersing some one-handed throws might help keep the engineer awake. I suspected that he tended to nod off if

I didn't surprise him occasionally. He was too smooth for me to catch him at it in any obvious way, though. Regardless of using one hand or two, we moved many logs each day for over a month. Then the skyline broke down.

A skyline has a cable with a carriage on it suspended between two spar trees. The carriage has chokers hanging from it that are used for pulling logs from one tree to the other. Our tree had one end of a skyline hung near its top, in addition to the heel boom hanging from it lower down. I had to disconnect the logs that came in on the skyline when I was not setting tongs. Thus, the word *chaser* appeared in my chaser second loader job title. The breakdown meant that we soon ran out of logs to load. The head loader and the engineer went on holiday, and Jonesy sent me to a different show.

Complications on a Spreader Bar Show

When Jonesy told me that I would be setting tongs on a spreader bar, I had different concerns than those I had when he was telling me about working on the heel boom. One concern derived from two older guys who had amused themselves in a previous camp by telling horror stories about running duplex loaders that used two tongs hanging from a spreader bar. Being a rabid collector of anything concerning logging, I was right there listening with both ears while they were telling their dramatic stories. The themes usually emphasized how easy it was to kill someone by accident, or on purpose when running such loaders. No doubt they were playing to the cheap seats with some of their tales, but their technical descriptions were realistic enough for me to swallow them whole. As the stories went, if one tong let loose while lifting a log, the loose tong could travel in an arc as the log fell and could kill you. According to the two old raconteurs, some engineers—watch out, kid—knew how to make tongs miss on purpose and occasionally used the knowledge. The motives behind the killings were the usual human ones, such as a partner needing a job during the great depression or someone wanting sex from another guy's wife or girlfriend. The spreader bar we were heading for had two tongs.

My second concern was more complicated. Jonesy was behaving oddly while assigning me the job. He was usually very straightforward in such situations. You know:

"Do this, and if you lose your balance, fall toward the rigging."

Or he would say I would catch on fast as he had when I mentioned my inexperience in setting tongs. But with this assignment, he was almost shuffling his feet while noting I would have a helper. Jeez, what was going on? I only had two hands hanging on my arms, and the tongs on the spreader bar were 15 feet apart. My uneasiness increased even more as it became apparent that having this helper would land me with more responsibility than usual. There just had to be a big hook in the situation somewhere. There proved to be two hooks. One was that my wages would stay the same. The other was a surprise.

Jonesy told me that I would be responsible for training the young person who would be helping. He was 17, and his family was having difficulty with him. (I was only 19 or 20 at the time, but the difference in experience between us was huge.) Jonesy gave me the impression that he did not have much choice in hiring the boy because his parents had a financial interest in the logging camp. I remember feeling nervous about working with a problem child, especially in the situation we were heading for. The 'duplex loader' worry I had picked up made me wonder just how dangerous the situation would be?

The crummy carrying us to the job site seemed to take longer than usual. No one said much, and the journey felt like we were entering a new space very different from skylines, heel booms, and high lead logging. Having just finished reading Conrad's "Heart of Darkness," combined with Jonesy's introduction to the job, had put me in a somewhat altered state.

Arriving at the worksite that the first morning, I saw a small loading machine, a D8 caterpillar, a pile of logs, and a small spar tree about 50 feet long. The spar tree leaned at an angle, and the 15-foot spreader bar, with tongs connected to each end by cables, hung above the stakes of the logging truck parked beneath it—the tongs were lighter than those on the first show I had been on. The engineer, who must have come up before us to maintain the machines, was standing beside the loader. He had been my bridge partner and would run both the D8 and the loading machine. Seeing a friendly face with a grin settled me down quite a bit.

Since the engineer couldn't run the Cat and hook behind it simultaneously, I would have to do it. Walking back into the bush, while he drove the cat, I would select logs, put chokers on them, and connect the chokers to the bullhook on the D8's winch line. When the D8 had pulled the logs to the landing, I would unhook them, and we would go back into the bush to get another load. I was no stranger to such a job and was looking forward to it. It might even be possible to get the helper to chase in the landing once he was broken in. Someone else unhooking the logs in the landing would save me the effort of walking from one place to the other. Things did work out that way to some extent, but, unfortunately, events in the other parts of the job seriously interfered with what we were doing. It will require a description of rigging and procedures to appreciate the situation.

There was a block near the top of the leaning spar tree through which a cable from the loading machine connected to the spreader bar with its tongs hanging from both ends. It allowed the engine to pull the bar toward the tree while lifting it, along with a log being held by the tongs. The lift was high enough for the log to clear the stakes on the logging truck. Another cable from the loading machine went through a block on the tree below the first one. It travelled past the pile of logs we would be loading from. Going through a block behind the pile, the cable returned and connected to the spreader bar. In this way, the second cable could pull the spreader bar back to the pile of logs where both tongs could be set on another log to be loaded.

The situation looked simple enough to me when I first saw it. The rigging worked, but it was slow. It didn't look all that dangerous, either. It took me some time to appreciate that the landing wasn't as innocuous as it felt. Even knowing the danger, I occasionally found it necessary to exert some effort in remaining alert. Sadly, the subtle nature of the situation completely misled my helper. His troubled state combined with his lack of experience was accompanied by a complete unwillingness to listen to me.

The seventeen-year-old was very negative on the job. He gave the impression of resenting where he was and resenting those of us who were there with him. We were a small crew and being responsible for him made keeping away from him impossible and telling him what to do a delight. Any suggestion or order elicited stubborn resentment. Even after explaining my safety concerns about the setting, his behaviour still forced me to keep pointing out potential hazards. I constantly had to tell him to preserve an acceptable distance from what was happening. He just did not seem to believe me and rebelled against it every time.

I wasn't sure at first, but it soon became apparent that my helper started moving closer to the truck when my back was turned forcing me to tell him to move back. I took the tactic to be his way of being smart and saying 'Up yours'.

As loading went on and nothing drastic happened, the young fellow appeared to become increasingly convinced he was right with every daring move he made. His contempt, and lack of trust were becoming prominent and growing steadily. I tried not to think about it too much, but it was sad, worrisome, and irritating. Ignoring it was becoming harder and harder to do.

Slow landing or not, things were going well on the production end. I even recall wondering, in a weak moment, if I was being overly cautious. But I did not drop the precautions I was taking. Persisting in walking further out from slowly moving logs and avoiding standing on a log that might move if another log hits it, were becoming difficult in the face of the young man's contempt. I knew he was wrong for not being more careful. I just didn't know what to do about his behaviour. It didn't help that the kid was bright enough to find fault with just about anything I said. With a bit of luck, the situation might have allowed more time for things to work out. Other people have gotten more time to learn how important it is to listen to front-line troops. Lord knows I had some. I kept watching him as much as I could, but our time had run out. What happened was probably inevitable. It may have even been lucky for us both in some ways.

After a week or two on the job, my fellow worker set his tong, and it came off after the engineer had lifted the log. It was something that could happen to either of us. He had learned to set tongs quite quickly and was doing the job reasonably well. His potential provided another part of my frustration in the situation. As one would expect, his end of the log dropped and hit the other logs below, then began to roll. The movement threw the loose tong in a powerful circle toward us. Our worksite had gone instantly from a place of safe, slow movements to quick and dangerous. Being back far enough, while not standing on any log that would move if hit, I reflexively looked and saw my fellow worker had stayed closer to the pile than I had. (Or, he had moved in as part of the game he was playing. To this day, I don't know which it was.) There was no time for him to move away or for me to do anything. I saw the flying tong hit him. Its arc was high enough to glance off the back of his hard hat, which deflected the blow sufficient for it to only knock him to the ground unconscious. Four or five inches lower, and he may well have been dead or disabled for life. God bless hard hats and a membership in the turtle club.

The problem child lay there badly dazed and shaken up for quite some time. He didn't say anything. The engineer, trucker, and I continued watching him carefully until he began trying to get up. We then helped him up and sat him in a safe place to recover.

None of us spoke. I do not know about the others, but I didn't know what to say. So, instead of talking, I waited until the engineer returned to the loading machine, then re-set the loose tong and finished loading the truck. It was a study in cooperation between the engineer and me and very slow going. But we persisted and eventually got the job done. When the load was ready, I sent the young fellow back to camp on the truck to get "checked out." He was shaky and still hadn't said a word.

Jonesy came up with the driver on the return trip to talk about what had happened. One theory was that it was essential to get the lad back into the situation as soon as possible after taking the hit. It was thought that the fear would develop and stay if one didn't. (Years later, I found research in psychology that gave some credence to this view. At the time of the accident, I was following what other, more experienced men had told me.) We considered bringing him back to continue the job but concluded he might be safer working at something else. The truck driver and the machine operator had known what was going on with the young man, and had been concerned about him, too. The four of us agreed the youngster just did not want to be there. And we would not be able to keep our eyes on him enough to keep him safe and do our jobs. Jonesy decided to put him to work on the booms where there might be a little less action.

The youngster was housed in the small married quarters with one of the families there. So, I did not get a chance to talk to him again. But, by all accounts, he was still unhappy and left for town after working another week or so.

Jonesy and I had gone on to finish the rest of the loading together on that fateful day. It was great. Sometimes we used two hands and sometimes only one. An outsider might have thought what Jonesy was doing was easy. But, to me, it was great to watch the grace and power in what he did. Working with him helped me to settle down and bleed off the remainder of my sick stomach and adrenaline high. We went back to camp together an hour early, too. On the way back to camp I said: "You know, Jonesy, you are so good with tongs that you can help me set them anytime." I think he may even have been a bit pleased with the semi-joke. Thanking me for the invitation to work together, he gracefully excused himself and sent me a new helper the next day. The helper was more experienced than the young fellow, and we easily finished the setting.

Burning Slash

When my new helper and I had finished the spreader bar show, we went with some others to burn a slash pile. It was the first time I helped burn such a pile, and it was proving to be quite a holiday. After lighting the pile, all we had done so far was stand ready in watchful inaction. With grub hoes and watering cans beside us, we were enjoying a wonderfully sunny day. As some wag suggested, all we needed were hot dogs to make our bliss complete. The comment spurred some ideas, and we decided to toast our sandwiches over the slash fire, not having any hotdogs. Toasting made them taste excellent, though they might not have been quite as good as those toasted during a cold rainy day. It would be hard for a cordon bleu chef to compete with them.

While gobbling our sandwiches, we suddenly noticed with complete surprise, followed by the rapid disappearance of our lackadaisical attitude, that the slash fire was spreading. Sprinkling cans and grub hoes in hand, we galvanized into action. We were losing ground until the logging road we travelled on, aided by a firebreak built on one side of the slash pile built by the D8 operator, contained the fire on two fronts, allowing us to concentrate on the other two directions.

After halting the spread of the fire, we noticed another emergency developing. Contrary to all our hopes, our situation had not gone unobserved by others. The realization came when we saw a group of grim-looking men in shiny white hats and clean clothing striding up the logging road toward us. Planes had flown over the ocean earlier but had not passed us by as we had hoped they would. Instead, they landed on the water, dropping off the group we saw walking toward us. The situation was to show some of Jonesy's characteristics: valour and eloquence under fire.

Upon the arrival of our visitors at the scene of our battle with the slash fire, a caucus began between Jonesy, who was smaller than them in all but physical size, and our guests. I can still see him holding forth on the benefits of his carefully constructed firebreak. He was magnificent while extolling how his prescience saved us from the fire that had started through some unexplained accident. It was a massive lie in all respects. Everyone knew who started the fire and where it burned, including our visitors. Maybe they would be able to let him off, however, if the uncomfortable facts of the situation remained undiscussed.

There is a principle here that seems to operate in many situations. It relies on the fact that ignoring some crimes that have worked out OK can be beneficial. After all, Jonesy had been careful and diligent in monitoring and fighting the resultant fire. It did not hurt that he delivered his arguments with incredible sincerity, either. I believed he may even have begun to sway them. Sadly, one singular fact compromised his valiant efforts.

During his delivery, I noticed one of the white hats looking at Jonesy's feet rather than his beatific and compelling face. It was an oddly neglectful behaviour on the part of our guest. So, despite being as entranced by Jonesy's performance as the others were, I found myself also glancing at his feet. Our hero's overwhelming emotion had left his giant foot standing on one of the red firebombs we had used to start the slash fire. I had never seen one before that day, but the white hat had. And, like me, he could see part of it poking out from under Jonesy's boot. It was the straw-that-broke-the camel's back, as the saying goes.

No doubt because of his magnificent performance, our guests only shut Jonesy's camp down for two days while making him pay us full wages. They dashed our hope of a paid holiday, however, when they explained our task would be to go through the whole claim in the hot sun. Carrying power saws, grub hoes, and watering cans, we were to cut, dig, and water any smoky bits we found. One can see another principle operating here—when you are working with someone who is committing a crime, and they are caught, you will be punished for not speaking up.

We found a significant number of smoky bits, primarily residing in the culled logs left on the claim. Their rotten cores often housed smouldering punk. We even exposed root systems that smoked in the air when we dug them up.

It proved to be another example of Jonesy's largeness of spirit that he didn't blame us for having to pay our total wages. He didn't even ask us for a discount. (Firefighting did not pay well back then, and one could be pressed-ganged right out of a saloon to do it.) Jonesy's equipment may not have been the best, and his ideas could be a bit dicey. His rigging could even be crook, as you will see. But there was seldom a comeback from him when things screwed up. He delivered our checks on time too.

Chasing and Hooking-On

My sojourn in the camp had been reasonably pleasant and exciting up until this time. There was no reason to feel things would be any different when he sent me chasing hooking-on at the skyline after burning slash. The chasing involved unhooking the chokers from the logs coming in from a logging crew back in the bush. Hooking-on meant putting chokers back on the logs to send them up the skyline to where they would make another pile to load from. The logs from the bush came in much faster than the skyline could take them away. So, very soon, I had built a huge pile—called a cold-deck pile—of them in the landing. The pile became so large that a big fan of logs developed at the back, becoming bigger and bigger as the days went by. The situation forced me to go out of sight from the engineer while unhooking them. He was an excellent engineer, and my being out of his view did not worry me too much. Luckily, he was good enough to help me survive a dire situation I got myself into.

The fanned part of the pile became quite high, and I had to climb up to get to where the logs were coming in. On one turn, I unhooked the first log easily, but the choker on the other log was stuck tightly underneath it. Usually, I would have gone back down to where I could see the engineer and signal him to lift the log and then drop it again to get a better lay for unhooking it. I could see, however, that there was just enough choker showing underneath the log that I might be able to release it even tight as it was.

Stepping down with one leg between the rest of the pile and the log, I felt a subtle movement that trapped my leg. Luckily, it did not go far enough to crush it, but I thought I could feel the bone flexing as the rigging jerked the choker. (One needed some slack to unhook the chokers, which meant it was necessary to lower the mainline. For a variety of reasons, one didn't lower the cable all the way, but just enough to provide the needed slack. That left belly in the mainline and which often swung back and forth tightening and loosening the chokers. Visualize moving a skipping rope back and forth.) Feeling the jerks on my leg, I was now wondering if the log would begin moving again.

Out of sight from the engineer, my only choice was to wait there for the log to roll and finish me off or for the engineer to appear and help. It was a time for wild fantasies accompanied by feelings of vast regret. I stood there bent over for what seemed like forever, having a few of both. Then, God bless his soul, who should appear during my turmoil, but my best friend of the moment, and forever, Charley the engineer.

"GAWD!" he shouted while peering around the pile, then slowly walking over.

Carefully climbing up the pile, Charley bent down and looked at my trapped leg and the stuck choker.

Charley: "Can you hook the choker back up?"

Me: "I think so. Why?"

Charley: "Well, I can lift the log off you. Or we can blow one long and get the crew in to put a safety line on it first. It's your call."

One long was bad news for everyone on the claim and they would all come running. I had only heard it twice before. Looking at the log trapping me and the pile above it, while wondering when the riggin-bobbing would stop, I said:

"Let me hook the choker up, and we'll have another look."

Hooking the choker up again wouldn't necessarily save me. It could even make matters worse by transferring a bit more of the bobbing to the log. If the log began moving, it would be heavy enough to pull the rigging down, leaving me as a smear on the side of the log pile. This was one of the previously mentioned fantasies I had been having. Luckily, things remained stable after the choker was re-connected. Charley and I stared at each other while silently contemplating what we had to do.

Speaking from my heart, I said to him, "Take the log off me, Charley."

It was an emotional time. Charley turned and went back to his machine leaving me to live or die by myself. I saw the cables slowly rising higher above me into "tightline." He lifted that log six inches off my leg without disturbing a hair. Scrambling down the side of the pile, despite the awesome bruise growing on my leg, was an enormous relief.

When the logging crew met us at the end of the day and asked about the delay, we didn't tell them. It was a magical moment between Charley and me. If there is a heaven, I know one man who should have gone there when his time came. Happily, Saint Peter is rumoured to let most west coast loggers in. He knows they will not be there long because of their migrating ways.

Charley and I were both aware that the landing we were working in was hazardous but, unknown to us both, we were now moving toward another even more terrifying event. The crew in the bush was logging from the same spar tree that the skyline was hanging on. As a result, it was challenging to find a safe place to stand while working in the landing. The problem became acute as the cold deck pile grew and spread out. Eventually, I was forced to stand in the bight of the cables and blocks operating in the situation.

The cables from the yarder that Charley was running were delivering the chokers to the logging crew back in the bush, then pulling the logs back to the spar tree. The mainline, which was the heaviest cable, hauled the logs to the spar tree. It travelled up from Charley's machine and through the mainline block hanging on the spar tree far above my head. As you may recall, a block is a big pulley that cables run through. This one was about 200 pounds. The situation might be seen as being similar to a bow and arrow. The log being pulled by the mainline and the yarder pulling the cable would be the ends of the bow. The cable would be the bowstring, and the two-hundred-pound mainline block would be the arrow. Because I had to stand in the bight of the cable, that arrow, the two hundred pound mainline block hanging above me was pointing in my direction. The strap that held the mainline block up on the spar tree would be the hand holding the bowstring as the huge tension of pulling the logs into the landing was applied. Imagine what would have happened if the strap had broken. It would have released a two-hundred-pound arrow in my direction.

The logging crew was struggling with the terrain. They were continually fighting hang-ups, even with the lift provided by the spar tree. Charley and I could not see them, but we could tell how difficult things were by the signals they were sending in, as well as by what the rigging and the yarding machine were doing. The massive yarder was pulling hard, then stopping with a slam as the logs hung up back in the bush. The crew was working out of sight behind a rock bluff where stumps left by the fallers were hanging up (stopping) the logs. The sudden stop pulled hard on the mainline block while shaking the spar tree. The 300-horsepower diesel pulling the mainline would roar, and the yarder would begin rising into the straps put over its skids to hold it in place. A single whistle signalling Charley to 'stop pulling' would come in, and the massive machine would slam back down with everything shaking. Then, other signals to pull back, stop, and slack line would come in. A delay would follow as the crew adjusted the chokers. The crew would then signal Charley to pull forward again. The fight went on and on, turn after turn—I still don't know why someone didn't blow those stumps. You can imagine the noise and stress with so much power applied and so many hang-ups occurring.

Suddenly there was silence. I could not hear a thing. Not conscious in any meaningful way, I slowly looked behind me and saw the two-hundred-pound mainline block about six feet away. It had buried itself in the frozen ground between me and Charley's yarder. The mainline cable, which remained trapped in the block also went over my head. One eye of the broken strap which had held the block to the tree was still on the block's gooseneck. A 200-pound projectile with a cable companion had just flown about a foot over my head. I saw Charley leap out of his chair with his mouth open. His seventy-two-year-old neck was swollen by stress marks. He looked like a rooster that was screaming rather than crowing. Looking at him from what felt like miles away, I heard only silence. There were no words. I was the standing undead, without even knowing what had happened.

We had unknowingly set the conditions that could kill me; a rigger had failed to swing blocks; someone had spliced an eye on the strap holding the mainline block wrong; and we were logging at diamond lead. Swinging blocks means moving blocks around the tree to keep the pull aligned to them. The way the eye of the strap holding the mainline block was spliced and not swinging the block froze it in one position on the spar tree. These errors meant that the massive stress being applied due to the hang-ups and pulling of the logs was placed primarily on one eye of the strap. As mentioned, we were logging at diamond, lead, which meant we were pulling logs from a direction that went nearly behind Charley's machine. The spar tree holding the mainline block was in front of his machine. Pulling at such an acute angle would increase the distance the block would travel out from the spar tree if it were to fall.

I was nervous about logging at diamond lead and aware of the need to stand off from the tree. But I believed I was standing a safe distance away if the block were to come down. In an oddly funny, or not so funny, way, I was correct. If I had moved closer to the tree, I would have been safe. The flying block would have killed me if I had been standing a bit farther out from the tree. The situation felt entirely arbitrary with a huge, potential payoff for me.

While I was looking at that block buried six inches into the frozen ground, something began changing in me. You would not have seen it by looking on the outside. But, for the first time in my life, I felt that something outside my control had prevented me from being killed. By this time, I had seen men killed or seriously injured, but it had always felt as if it was due to them having done something wrong. A chaser had turned his back on the wrong log; a faller had failed to consider the top of the tree that came back on him; a construction worker had tied back the guard on his Skilsaw to cut a vertical post. A man had been felled by a blow in a fight and his head hit a curb. I had made errors myself; just think of how I blithely stepped between that log and the others in the pile. Somehow, however, the present mistake had a different effect than the others I had experienced. Now I was looking at certain death right in the eye and felt that my survival in the situation was due to the intervention of something other than myself and those around me. Most people have an explanation for this. Some might explain my survival as chance or due to the intervention of God. A physicist with sufficient motivation could explain how various factors acted to make the block miss me. However, the results from physics in such cases had gone the other way with other men many times over. So, in a way, their explanation would be of cold comfort to me. I accepted the physics of the situation, but my time was not up on that day, and I am still not sure why.

Even if I was no longer feeling normal, I probably behaved in a way that looked like I was. The hook and rig (high rigger) came to re-hang the block in the spar tree with a better strap. He asked me to splice the new strap and chase for him while he was up the tree re-hanging the block. Sending things up to the rigger while relaying his signals to the engineer was another part of being a chaser. Helping correct the problem settled me down. You can be damned sure I spliced that strap correctly.[7]

I suspect there were private conversations, but no one talked about what happened when they were around me. I did see guys looking at me out of the side of their eyes occasionally. Charley, of course, remained Charley, one of the finest, but he was not talking, either. Later, he did help me figure out how close that block had come to my

---

[7] When one splices eyes in a strap, it is important to ensure that the individual strands of the cable protruding from the splices, called the feathers, are facing in the same direction so the strap can move around the tree. If the hook and rig goes up to swing the block and the feathers bind into the wood of the tree, you better be ready to run before he gets down.

head. We were all quiet. It wasn't a good silence; mistakes had been made.

A Fateful Plan

Winter had been slowly coming on. So far, it was just cold with the occasional skiff of snow falling on the frozen ground. Logging would stop in many places on the coast as more serious snowfalls appeared. So, we were all thinking about getting some time off. I would probably help mail carriers deliver Christmas mail in place of collecting pogey. Each would pay the same but delivering mail would get me out of the house.

While I, and the others, were having such warm, fuzzy thoughts, however, Jonesy had disappeared from camp to meet his friends and was creating some warm fuzzy ideas about a project of his own.

He and his friends were meeting at their usual bar when the plan began emerging. Confidential, though reliable, sources told me conception occurred while imbibing kegs of beer. The scene must have involved much positive speculation,, since it resulted in transferring $3,500 to one of Jonesy's "friends" before the end of the evening. He came back to camp almost as enthusiastic about his new idea as he was about the bridge game.

Stepping off the bomber, Jonesy immediately started haranguing some of us, his semi-loyal crew, to share in his excitement. It is a sad commentary that we weren't as enthused as he was. We were tired, having been in camp quite a while by then, and the way things had been going were worrisome. In the end, we went along with his plan, even though the project sounded like quite an 'uphill' struggle. (The word 'uphill' is intended as a bit of an in-joke between you and me, as you will see. I should have used 'downhill' instead.) What had finally carried the day was the impending camp closure due to snowfall and the prospect of earning additional money. Jonesy's enthusiasm made the proposal sound exciting and feasible. In retrospect, it seems funny how doomed something can be with so much evidence supporting its practicality. Even at this late date, I am forced to confess to having a bit of pride about being there through it all.

Jonesy's "friends" in the bar had told him about an abandoned show, which had an A-frame on a raft on the ocean, along with a yarder. (An A-frame is a type of spar tree made by tying two large trees together, making an 'A' shaped structure. The middle of the 'A' is also a log, which helps the framework keep its physical integrity as well as allowing equipment to be hung from it.)

One friend said another yarder was left on a plateau above the raft. It had logged much of the country around the table, sending the logs down to the A-frame along a skyline. (A skyline, as you may recall, has a cable suspended between two trees with a carriage carrying chokers that travels on it.) According to Jonesy's friends, who were proving to be a fount of fascinating information, the skyline cable was still there lying on the trail the logs followed coming down. In a moment of honesty that sometimes happens in a bar, one friend, who had recently passed the show on a tug, told him sadly that the A-frame and the donkey (another name for yarder) that had been on the raft were no longer there. However, he went on to say that the raft was still there, as was the yarder on the plateau above it, along with much of its jewelry. The presence of the jewelry may well have been the deciding factor for Jonesy. It meant guy lines, cables, many kinds of blocks of assorted sizes and shapes, tree jacks, tree plates, straps, cables, shackles, and other arcane stuff significant to loggers. None of those things came cheaply, even in those days. Together, these facts implied an impressive amount of value was present at the scene. A small price of $3500, in the face of such riches, must have looked like an excellent deal to Jonesy. Undoubtedly, this rosy picture was helped by consuming additional kegs of beer.

It was true that there were many apparent benefits to going along with Jonesy and his view of the riches to be gained. There was a good chance he would pay us, too. Jonesy had stood the test of time on that, as you know. There appeared to be only a few minor impediments standing against the venture by decision time. One was that the yarder on top was 2200 feet above the ocean, but that fact didn't sink in until we looked directly up at it from the ocean. Jonesy's presentation concerning the project was also very compelling. I can still hear him to this day.

Here is a sample of what one of his presentations might have sounded like:

"It will be easy," Jonesy would say.

(He means tough. Maybe it will be easy for him.)

"We…"

(Substitute "you," meaning 'us'. In fact, always make such substitutions, you will be closer to the truth. Watch out for words like 'only', or 'all', and 'can', too.)

"…can pull the skyline around a stump, then hook it to the back of the yarder to snub it on the way down. Using the donkey—another word for yarder—we bring from camp on the raft, we can pull the yarder on the plateau down to the raft we have towed over the show (job site). We can then tow it back to camp. The setting is only a couple of hours away by tug. We will have to string some straw line, but many blocks are still up there, and we won't even have to carry one up. All we'll have to do is find a decent tail hold for the block."

It all sounded so plausible. Straw line is a small cable about five sixteenths of an inch in diameter or even a bit lighter. We could carry the line in coils on our shoulders or pull it up by hand. The light cable would pull up heavier lines strong enough to move the yarder down to the raft. We could use the skyline cable left lying along the path the logs had followed to stop the yarder on the plateau from running away while we were pulling it down the hill. What could possibly go wrong?

Following preparatory trips by Jonesy and a tug to get the raft, tow it back to camp, and put a camp donkey on it, we set out for the show very early the following day. It was pitch black outside but kind of pleasant sitting in the warm cabin of the tug. There was even a mild sense of going on an adventure to get the riches Jonesy had described so eloquently. A thermos full of coffee helped, too. Only a small red light and a dim yellowish one relieved the darkness in the boat. The red light was on the sonar. It occasionally winked in time with changes going on in the water beneath us. The yellowish light illuminated the sonar's screen.

It was the first time I had seen the man running the tug. He proved to be the engineer who would run the donkey during the forthcoming events. After a long, restful ride, he quietly announced we were nearing our destination. At the same time, the sonar, which I had been watching with great interest, began showing the ocean bottom disappearing beneath us. The flashing light and the rapid disappearance of the ocean bottom left me with an uneasy feeling. Our prospective worksite also had a daunting aspect in the early morning light. The overcast sky was sprinkling a bit of snow, and the temperature was hovering around a chilly 12°F. The country went 2,200 feet down from the plateau at the top. It travelled in three very steep sections. Standing there, we could now appreciate the enormity of the distance. There were narrow, reasonably flat transitions between the vertical sections. The steep face of the final drop above the raft, which was the shortest drop, looked like it went straight down into the unimaginable depths the bottom had disappeared to on the sonar. A small hump of rock on the edge of the flat spot at the top of the face seemed innocuous in the morning light. Later, it would be of grave importance in the unfolding adventure.

Happily, the climb up to the first flat spot was not all that bad. The wood coming down during logging had scoured a pathway we could scramble up. The other two steps that eventually reached the yarder and the spar tree on the plateau above were longer, and both were also very steep. In a similar fashion to the first rise, the best way up meant following the pathway that the logs had Travelled on their way down. The route was rough but manageable. We would often bend over with one hand on the ground while carrying stuff up, but we could rest on the two narrow flats between the steep parts. The place was a complete bastard while appearing to be just about ideal for what we wanted to do.

The first glitch was that no straw line was left on the yarder up above. We had expected the big cables to be gone, but it would have been nice to find the straw line still there. Its absence meant we had to carry coils of straw line up the steep rises. The yarder on the raft carried some straw line in its drum, which we pulled out. But it was considerably shorter than the 4,400 feet or so required to get up to the yarder on the plateau and back down again to pull the other cables. There was a certain amount of grumbling at the situation, as you might imagine.

We had begun transporting the coils of cable, and the going was proving to be about as tough as we had imagined it would be. As we struggled, we could hear Jonesy yelling at us from where he had positioned himself close to the nice warm donkey engine. So far, his complaints that we were going too slowly had been easy for us to ignore.

Suddenly, there was the peppering sound of hundreds of tiny pellets hitting all around us, followed by the booming of a shotgun. We all looked back in disbelief. Jonesy was shooting at us with a shotgun. Here is what it sounded like:

"Come on, you bastards! Get your miserable asses up there! Bang! Bang! Bang! Hah! Hah! HAH!"

After standing there with our mouths open for one or two stunning moments as Jonesy kept trying to help us move faster, we then showed our usual class by accelerating rapidly up the hill in shocked surprise, stopping to sit down only when we were utterly winded. No doubt our sitting would grieve Jonesy, but he would have to climb quite a distance to catch us, or to shoot us, for that matter. He would also have to get another crew, even if he only maimed us. Oddly enough, we appeared to take being shot at as just part of the job. We even did a bit of swearing and chuckling while sitting there catching our breath.

I was going down the hill for another coil of straw line when I found Jonesy lying on the ground near the top of the second run. It looked like he was trying to decide whether or not to have a heart attack. Dissatisfied with our acceleration after shooting at us, he had begun carrying a coil up himself. Undoubtedly, he intended to show us how he wanted it done, much like how he had demonstrated setting tongs. He may even have been trying to shame us into moving more quickly. Perhaps my dispassionate attitude was a bit unfair. But he had shot at us, which made his having a heart attack seem funny. Where do these things stop?

Looking at him lying there, I became fascinated. So, instead of continuing down the hill, I stopped to enjoy the sound of his breathing. There were some differences in tonality, but it sounded a bit like the roaring noise he made while jumping on the floor at the bridge game.

Instead of leaving him to his task of expiring, I went over and took the coil off his shoulder, saying, "Come on, Jonesy."

I put the coil on my shoulder and carried it the rest of the way up the hill for him. Did I experience too much pleasure while listening to his breathing or when carrying his coil? Jonesy was getting older, and there had probably never been a day when he could not have done what he was trying to do. He was now carrying 50 pounds of excess body weight, along with 30 more years than me. I could have been a little less of a smart ass. We all have regrets, and that is one of mine. At this stage, however, our pleasures had only just begun.

It was hard, cold work, but everything went well after carrying up the coils of straw line. Dropping the spar tree on the plateau was exciting, and we accomplished it without serious problems. We had connected all the cables we needed to pull everything down to the raft. We had the skyline cable to stop everything from running away. Pulling slack to put the skyline around the enormous old stump we selected for it to run around and snub the yarder involved some grunting and pulling, but it was soon achieved. The stump was all of seven or eight feet across, and the consensus was it would never pull out. We were right, too. But putting the skyline around the stump, rather than running it through a block hung from it, would prove to be a significant error. We didn't have a strap long enough to put around the stump. So, we couldn't hang a block for the skyline to run through. I don't know why we didn't think to make a strap. Lord knows there was enough cable lying around Attaching all the jewelry to the back of the yarder was hard labour, but it saved us from the more arduous labour of carrying it all down by hand. Things were looking like a success in the making.

The day we went to move the machine down from the plateau dawned with the first sunshine we had seen in three days. Excitedly arranging ourselves along the skyline road, we ensured we were far enough away from it to be safe while still seeing everything. Sunshine made the visibility good enough to know every detail as things unfolded. Luckily, one of my fellow workers and I were standing about halfway up the mountain, which was where things began to get fascinating.

The final phase had started well, and after a heavy struggle with static friction, the yarder began moving over the edge of the plateau. I had an odd feeling watching it as it started. It was almost as if I had not believed what we were doing would work and then was surprised that it did. As the yarder moved quickly toward the first narrow flat area, we saw it begin to slow. The diesel below us sounded louder but we could see nothing wrong. Then, as the yarder moved over the edge of the flat spot and into the next drop, it slowly stopped. In disbelief, we watched as the side nearest to us began rising off the ground. As it rose, we saw the other side start following. There were enormous forces at work. Up and down the mountain, all of us began shouting and waving our arms and hardhats, trying to get the donkey on the raft to stop pulling. But things went too far before we successfully got the engineer to see us and stop pulling. The skyline cable snubbing the load broke where it was connected to the yarder, and the yarder began running away.

Later, we found out that the snubbing line had cut into the stump we had strung it around. It eventually created a slot deep enough to freeze the cable in place. So, we ended up pulling the yarder from the front while holding it in place at its back. The machine could go nowhere but up until something gave way. One side came up before the other because we had hooked the back and front lugs on opposite sides. Any hope for the yarder stopping disappeared when we saw the jewelry being pulled behind it begin to move. My fellow worker and I stood there in stunned silence as the whole mess accelerated down the steep skyline road. Finally, confirming the unrelenting nature of what we were seeing, the guy beside me reflectively said something that sounded like:

"Eeeeyuhhhh. Uh huh."

After sharing another brief pause, we began laughing like a couple of morons. It was a moment of total helplessness and acceptance. Do you recall the knob I saw at the top of the first rise when we arrived at the worksite? It was the only thing standing between the yarder, now running freestyle down the hill and the raft with the engineer and Jonesy on it. Jonesy and the engineer were watching a freight train weighing 20 plus tons aiming right at them. Furthermore, the train appeared to be accelerating all the way. Who can blame them for diving into the ocean? Seeing them go in only increased the hilarious nature of what was going on for the rest of us. We were all the butt of a cosmic joke. It was perfect slapstick with a bigger stick than usual.

The galloping yarder hit the rock knob with a massive impact. Its back end went up, looking like it would go over, then it stopped and came back down with a mighty crash. The rock hump had proven to be just high enough to halt the yarder in its tracks. I had feared the curved ends of its skids would allow the machine to go over. Even Jonesy couldn't come up with a plan to get it off the bottom of the inlet if that happened. In retrospect, the outcome was about the best we could have hoped for. As the machine landed back down, the jewelry, still travelling, began piling up behind it. The resulting conglomeration that built up resembled a Gordian knot ten or twenty feet high. There were many things in that knot, including the 300-foot guy lines that had held up the spar tree. The debris picked up on the way down was also impressive. Even the gods would have some trouble untangling it all. It was their kind of joke, and they would undoubtedly leave us to do the untangling.

I have little memory of what we did after the machine stopped. Jonesy and the engineer were able to swim back to the raft in the frigid water. We would have had one heck of a time getting to them fast enough if they failed to make it. Thawing them out by wrapping them in blankets from emergency stores on the tug, then sitting them close to the warm yarder engine, which was still running, we began looking over our situation. The four of us remaining ambulatory then began pulling the machine, along with the Gordian knot, onto the raft. Later, two of us went up and chopped the skyline out of the stump on the plateau, and we loaded that, too. All four of us seemed to be working in a mental daze. The trip back to camp that night was a long, quiet one. Still looking worse for wear, the engineer ran the boat, with Jonesy sitting next to him in the mirror and fug. There was satisfaction mingled with our fatigue as we sat there, along with some surprise that everything was on the raft. I remember sneaking the occasional glance at the darkened windows in the tug as if I could not believe it was there. From time to time, there was a soft rustle in the gloom as one or two of the others turned their bodies to do the same thing.

Leaving

Now I was walking down the same stiff leg I had walked up when entering camp. Jonesy had told me I had to go. He didn't appear angry as much as saddened, and he didn't say the word "fired." But it is what was happening all the same. I was being blamed for the mistake of another man. What feelings of anger, guilt, and shame were in me during that walk! They would become background feelings when I had calmed down enough to analyze the situation and my role in it. Jonesy hadn't burned bridges, either, but had left me a road back. When the agency told me that I could return to his camp, I found out about that. In a way, I was failing both myself and Jonesy by simply walking away. So, why didn't I fight? Part of it was that I felt guilty about not suggesting to the man responsible to ask someone else about what he was doing. I didn't know the answer to the question he asked me. So, technically, saying I didn't know what he should do and telling him so meant I was blameless. But I didn't think about encouraging him to ask someone else, especially the head loader. He and the head loader were at odds, but the suggestion should have been made. So, I hadn't helped, and part of the blame was still mine. Another reason for not arguing came from being sick at heart and not wanting to be there anymore. How does one know when to leave?

Jonesy is gone now, and I think about him from time to time. I mourn how things ended and think about how far my responsibility had to go in that final situation. Then I remember seeing him while he was trying to talk guys into pulling just one more block or cable out of that Gordian knot. I remember his enthusiasm for ideas, commitment to them, and ability to inspire others. Something was heartening about him getting up after failing to carry that coil up that awful side hill. He hadn't quit, and I felt happy, as well as a bit sad when I thought of it. Sometimes, memories of working in Jonesy's camp have helped me encourage someone or helped me pick myself up on my better days.

A Prayer

I hope there are machines to move, and riggin' to do it with, where you ended up Jonesy. There should be a block with a strap hanging on a stump to carry the snubbing line. It will prevent the inevitable cutting into the stump that will happen if you don't. You might consider moving a machine more gradually than the one we pulled from the plateau that day. I hope your skylines are long enough and you swing blocks on spar trees early enough. You can keep setting the occasional tong one-handed, but it might help if you use two most of the time. There should be a saloon to plan in with your friends. And there should be an adequate supply of kegs full of beer to go with it. Get whoever runs the show where you ended up to put big pads on the bumper of your Cadillac and any bridge abutments, just in case you decide on a re-match. A governor on your vehicle might help. Maybe there will be a bridge game for your evenings, and lambs, like I was, for you to terrorize. I hope the floors you jump on are more robust. I recommend they put blanks in your shotgun after the ideas begin to flow; the money changes hands, and you go out to follow your plan!

THE BOSS

The Boss was massive when we first saw it covered in snow and surrounded by crystal clear air at a temperature hovering near minus 40 degrees. It was so clear that its presence seemed to be enlarged as it towered over us. It's odd, but I don't remember much about the mountain's appearance. It remains as just a vast, brooding shape in my memory, a visceral background spectre.

The construction camp we lived in, and the buildings we would be working on, were all located on the side of the spectre, as were the entry to the mine drilled into its bowels and the mill being built 120 feet below. I can still feel how cold the air was, with any wind making it unbearable. The thousands of ice spicules with sunlight flashing off them that occasionally floated around us are still present in my mind. I can hear the diesel engines left running at night so they wouldn't freeze. Their exhausts added huge white billows under the camp lights. But there is no image of The Boss itself. While we were on the job, what registered were close-ups of the mountain and the building site.

We were a cladding crew of four sent to cover the roofs of three huge buildings at a mine, as well as the track shed projecting from the mine's entrance and connecting 120 feet up the side of the mill being constructed below. The buildings looked like giant military Nissan or Quonset structures with huge, curved roofs and fifteen-foot vertical walls. The job was a tough one, located in a challenging environment. Only two of us made it to the end. The first to go was a man who didn't make it to our worksite on the second morning. We never saw him again. Rumour had it that the police had shown up in camp the evening before and taken him away. That left three of us to do the work.

Laying felt on the roofs might sound hazardous, and I suppose it was. But it didn't seem all that hard or dangerous back then. Felt isn't very slippery and, after laying the first couple of rows by standing on staging at the edge of the roof, we had an excellent surface to work on. Nailing two by fours to the roof and supporting our feet, we could work our way up each side, rolling out the felt and stapling it as we went. It was hard work, but the solid footing reduced the stress, and we made good time. The corrugated iron was an entirely different kettle of fish. It was tough to stand on; some might even say impossible. It was slipperier than any ice I had been on. Ice-covered with a thin film of water would be close. Crawling around at an angle on the track shed roof or hanging in buckets while installing steel side sheets over 100 feet up would also be a delight

We began by covering the roofs of the buildings. It took three thirty-foot corrugated iron sheets to cover each row of the rooftops on the three buildings. We installed the side sheets on the three roofs first, then went back to install the cap sheets. The cap sheets ran down the middle of the buildings while overlapping the side sheets on each side. Handling the iron sheets took two of us and proved the most difficult to put on. The side sheets could be slid up the sides of the roof from staging, and we had sound footing on the stage itself or the felt. The two of us held the cap sheets two or three feet in from the end and walked them down the roof to install them. Where we held the sheets was a compromise, allowing us to control them while keeping them high enough to clear the roof's curvature as we walked. Our feet were still on the felt underlay we had put down before, but they were close to the tops of the sheets on each side. Those side sheets were extremely slippery and hazardous in the cold, something we were very aware of.

Things were going well, and we were close to half done on the cap on the first building. The chap I was installing with was a good guy, as well as a hard worker. He even had a sense of humour, though he was kind of a fuss-budget. I remember hearing him repeating that we had to be careful and not step on a side sheet. Meanwhile, I watched where I put my feet while listening to his warnings and thinking it was just his way to worry about things.

Suddenly, the sheet we were carrying shook violently and began laying back on me. Being driven backward and down onto the roof, I tried to make made sure I fell onto the felt while controlling the sheet as best I could on my way down. (Controlling a sheet can be an important safety issue on a roof. Running free it has the potential to go anywhere and be hazardous.) After landing on the felt with my legs and hips under the sheet, I looked for my partner. I couldn't see where he went because of the curvature of the roof, and my first thought was that he was lying down like me. Then, with a shock, I realized I should be able to see him with my head raised the way it was. Feeling sick inside, I knew he had to have gone off the roof. We had lost our second man. All I could do was lie there and control the sheet. Others would have to help him.

The camp ambulance arrived quickly. I watched the first-aid men get out of the back carrying a stretcher, then run toward the building and disappear. The minutes dragged by as I continued lying there holding my sheet, feeling sick and wondering what was going on. Finally, the first-aid men reappeared carrying the stretcher with my workmate lying on it. I was relieved to see his face was uncovered.

After they put my co-worker in the back of the ambulance, it immediately drove away. Everything happened very fast. But it felt like a long time went by before someone came to help me with the sheet I was holding. Later, I found out my fellow worker had taken out the staging on his way down before falling the final 15 feet onto some lumber piled on the ground. Hitting the stage and stack of lumber may have saved his life. I never did see the injured man again, though I found out later that he recovered after spending a couple of years in and out of hospitals. Now there were only two of us to finish the job, my boss the sheet metal mechanic, and me,

We were on a big job, there was no relief in sight, and construction on the mill was behind schedule. The crews were high-balling to beat the band, and all the heavy equipment was constantly in motion. The fact was significant because the first task we faced after the accident was finishing the caps on the three roofs. The three of us had pulled up enough sheets to finish the first roof using two vice grips and a rope. We now had to get two piles of cap sheets up onto the two remaining roofs. If anything passes for humour in this story, it is how we solved the problem. It started with my boss saying he would see if the superintendent, the chief deity on the job, could spring us a crane to do the task.

He had been gone a long time when I heard equipment on the road. Curious, I went out into the wind from my hiding place to have a look. It's crucial at this point to provide a few pertinent facts. Being a newcomer to this camp, I wore a white hard hat with a decal showing my affiliation. Later, I found out that only foremen, or others occupying even more lofty heights, wore such white hard hats on the job site. It was also true that I had no reluctance about signalling machines, having worked around various kinds. Combine these facts with the pressing need for a crane to lift the sheets, and you might see why I adopted the approach I did.

It wasn't unusual for heavy equipment to be running near us. The road they were using to go down to the mill under construction below turned off close to where we were working. I had seen all sorts of equipment go down there. But, this time, when I saw a crane with a complete crew coming down the road toward the turn-off, I immediately began signalling them to come ahead. Seeing me signalling and wearing my white hard hat, they continued past the turn without a pause. Stopping the crane in front of me, the crew chief, who was also wearing a white hat, walked toward me while sizing me up on the way.

Looking me directly in the eyes with his steely set, he asked, "What do you need?"

Undaunted and looking right back with my own steely set, I replied, "I need those two stacks of sheets put on the cradles built on top of those two buildings."

He thought about the situation for an instant, then, not saying a word, he just turned around and got busy.

No doubt about it, they were an impressive crew! Turning off the road, they quickly dropped pads between the two buildings, then put sheet piles one and two on roofs one and two while doing so without any sweat or wasted motion. Up went the pads again in jig time and, after turning around, down they went to the mill site below. It was great to watch. I didn't even have to help them put on the straps.

Quite some time passed before my boss showed up, shaking his down-turned head and saying,

"Bad news! Bad news! I couldn't get a crane."

Seeing me standing there while saying nothing, he noticed the two piles of sheets weren't on the ground.

"Where in the hell are the sheets?" he asked.

"You were gone so long I carried them up onto the roofs," I answered.

My boss didn't hurt my feelings by commenting about my physical abilities. He did, however, require an immediate, detailed explanation. Listening intently while not interrupting, he held an impassive gaze as I told him how I thought a crane coming down the road was the one he had gotten for us. After hearing about the efficient dropping of the sheets on roofs one and two, and taking a moment to process, he erupted with a litany of repetitive expostulations. "Expostulations" might not be the best word to use here, but a big word might make things sound better than they were. He called on many kinds of deities, mothers, and my person—in creative ways. Eventually, the sounds he was making became a diminuendo whining, accompanied by continual rubbing of his shaking head.

"I don't know what to do! I don't know what to do," he kept moaning.

Then, impaling me with his dilated pupils—no doubt dilated from looking into a murky future—he directed a pointed question at me:

"What am I going to do at the all-trades meeting tonight when the push finds out *you* commandeered a crane?"

I hadn't, in fact, commandeered the crane. Previous experience told me that doing so could be trouble. There was a definite feeling of desperation growing around the two of us as we looked for a way out of our predicament. The source of our problem was clear. I mean, add it up; huge job behind schedule; high-balling crews; day and night running of heavy equipment; refusal of help to a sub-trade by a super under enormous pressure; millions of dollars at stake. I wasn't going to say it out loud, but my boss's ass was grass, and probably mine was, too.

Suppressing an almost overwhelming impulse to giggle as an epiphany struck, I blurted out, "Stand up before the topic is raised at the meeting and tell everyone how you appreciate the wonderful cooperation you have received on the job despite being new here."

I don't know if he had the balls to do it, but he got out of the meeting still on his feet. I think the reaming he received from our employer about the additional expense for the crane might have been worse. We probably weren't fired because no one sane would take our place. And we were able to finish installing the two roofs in good time. Then we went on to cover the track shed. Naturally, there was a minor glitch.

The sheets to cover the roof of the shed, which had been delivered in good time, turned out to be too long and extended too far beyond the edge of the roof. I can still see my boss walking up the road to make a phone call. His shoulders were slumping a bit when he walked. They were slumping even more when he told me we'd have to cut them shorter. At first, we tried using a circular saw, but the saw and its blades weren't very good. Cutting the sheets with them was very slow, and we had a long track shed to cover.

My boss eventually hit on the idea of burning the ends off with an acetylene torch. Sharing the task equally, we were over half-done before quitting work that evening.

The following day, feeling like we had a terrible case of flu, we staggered to the first aid shack. It was a treat listening to the first aid attendant. Maybe he wasn't quite as big as The Boss, but he was indeed as big as an average mountain, and he was much louder than The Boss.

"You complete fucking idiots!" he serenaded us. "You poisoned yourselves with the fumes from the zinc coating on the iron."

"What can we do?" we bleated.

"Drink lots of milk, pray, and continue working!" he snarled as he went back to more meaningful work.

I guess he was aware of the time challenge facing the super. Not having time to pray, we drank milk and went back to work. The milk even seemed to help a bit. Back at the job, with our tails in a suitable position, we looked at the circular saw, the sheets, and the torch. Seeing that we didn't have that many more sheets left to cut, my boss said, "Fuck it!"

Grabbing a particle mask, he added, "I'm going to cut the rest with the torch."

I did my half using a mask, too. Yup, same poison. I'd like to blame him, but in all honesty, I was glad he decided to use the torch—you had to be there to appreciate our desperation. After drinking a few gallons of milk, we began covering the roof of the track shed the next day.

Covering that shed was tough going with only the two of us, but we persevered and made good time. Oddly enough, apart from being poisoned, my most vivid memory from this part of the job was putting our gloves in our pockets and having the screws sticking to them in the cold weather. We never held a screw or nail with bare fingers. After pulling a glove out of our pocket with the fasteners sticking to it, we turned it back and forth while driving the screw or hitting the nail without removing our hand from inside the glove. It was tricky to avoid a hammer hit on a finger or catching the glove in the screw threads as we were driving them. But, by the time we were working on the track shed, we had a lot of practice. I don't believe we once hit a finger or caught a thread.

After completing the track shed roof, we took a day to load up and headed out. Feeling our trials were pretty much behind us, we looked forward to getting home for Christmas. What can I say? We were a tad optimistic in our outlook. Leaving the Boss with a few tons of iron on the back of the truck and with me driving brought us into a difficulty we didn't see coming.

We were on a slight grade a few miles from camp, heading toward what was easily a 1000-foot descent in several switchbacks, when I felt the traction go away. I was only doing about 20 miles per hour but started losing control even when gently trying to steer. Braking the truck proved to be next to impossible. Sometimes I could feather the brakes slightly, but it was too easy to start moving toward the side of the road. Even trying to shift down was a bad idea. The truck would begin wandering as soon as I tried to depress the clutch. I had never felt anything quite like it. The bind we were in was completely unexpected. Earlier, we had both met the chap who drove the van carrying food supplies and mail to the camp. He had told us he drove the road at high speed.

In the end, all I was able to do was maintain a low speed while steering very carefully. As the switchback was coming closer and closer, it became evident that we were probably going too fast to make it through. Panic began creeping up my spine as I realized that

I had no idea what to do. In desperation, I told my partner what was going on, adding in as normal a voice as I could that I thought he should bailout. He didn't respond. When I repeated myself, insisting more forcefully that he should think about getting out, he still didn't say or do anything. It was a wrench moving my eyes that were glued fixedly to the road, but, sneaking a glance, I saw him staring straight ahead with a chalky face and his hand white-knuckled on the door handle. He was frozen. Maybe he would get out of the truck if I did, and maybe he wouldn't. There was no sign he had even heard me. Not knowing what to do, I considered crashing the truck. But we were getting awfully close to the turn and, if I tried, we might lose control entirely and slide over the cliff. Conditions were that slippery. My mind went back to the thought of bailing out of the truck myself, but I just couldn't leave him or the truckload of steel. A fatalistic feeling began coming over me.

The time it took me to decide to try and get through the switchback felt like years. Then I felt calm and somehow removed from it all. I kept reassuring myself that the guy driving the camp van had gotten through the switchback while trying to forget that he didn't have tons of steel on the back of his van when he did. At the same time, I was using the steering wheel and brakes to slow the truck and bump it as close as possible to the side of the road where the drop-off would be. My idea was to turn into the curve at the slowest speed possible while building up snow on the side of the road next to the drop-off. Maybe piling up the snow would hold us away from the precipice enough to get us around the corner. Sneaking a glance in the mirror across from me, I saw the duals beginning to slide sideways and start piling up snow toward the drop-off while trying to turn the truck. We made it. Having a brief chance to look while we were straightening to come out of the corner, I could see the slide marks. It appeared that some of the snow we plowed went over the edge. It was that close.

Getting through the corner put us on an excellent line to the next one. Our situation improved again when we drove at an angle into the shallow ditch next to the road on the side opposite the drop-off. Our hitting the bank at an angle at the head of the next switchback slowed us down further. The impact with the bank also helped us bounce back onto the road as we entered the straight. From that point, getting through the rest of the switchbacks became a matter of maintaining a slow speed while not doing anything too dumb.

After reaching the bottom of the mountain, I turned to my fellow traveller and said, "Fuck was that ever close!"

Slowly turning toward me, he replied, "What?"

He had no memory of what we had gone through. He didn't even remember me telling him to get out of the truck twice. With a growing sense of unreality, I stopped trying to convince him about what we had been through and concentrated on driving. As things turned out, the difficulties on the trip weren't over.

Stopping for coffee and a piece of pie at a small café about 30 miles from The Boss, we switched drivers. We then made good time until we saw a body on the side of the road. Refusing to pull over, my partner drove by. Admittedly, I had some reservations about stopping, too, but I just couldn't pass by and ignore a body that might still be alive. Finally, agreeing to have a look, my partner pulled over. He said that he would look after the truck. He was pissed and told me he would wait while I walked back. The closer I came to the body, the more afraid I was of what I might see. There could be an awful mess if the person had been shot or hit by a vehicle. The body hadn't looked misshapen as we drove by, but it was a few feet off the road with its face turned away from us. Reaching it, I could see the figure wasn't very heavily dressed. I rolled him onto his back. He looked like a mature First Nation man. He didn't appear to be injured, but there was a powerful smell coming from him that stood me back a half-step. The dominant odours were liquor and vomit. He was completely passed out but still breathing.

Standing there, while trying to think, I didn't know what to do. We were unfamiliar with the country we were in, and we were in the middle of nowhere, to boot. The café where we had eaten was fifteen miles back, and the mine was another thirty, or so, beyond that. The next town going in our homeward direction was about forty or fifty miles further on. It was snowing lightly with a temperature close to zero F. The man could die of exposure if we left him.

When I had finally trudged back to the truck, I asked my partner to take him with us. He said the man couldn't ride in the cab, and there just wasn't room in the back. Kicking it around, we settled on going back to the café to ask how to find help. At least we might be able to do something so the man wouldn't die. Seeing the fellow hadn't moved as we passed by on our way back, we continued on. My partner, who was still pissed off and wanting to disassociate himself from the whole mess, wouldn't go into the café with me. Shaking a bit, I went in by myself and asked the man behind the counter if I could use their phone. He asked what I wanted it for.

Hearing the whole story, the proprietor said, "Oh hell, we lose three or four of them that way around this time every year."

Not knowing what to say, I just stood there with my mouth open.

Finally, he said, "I don't know what I can do or who to call."

His response sounded reasonable, but I had the impression he was feeling put upon and didn't care much about what was happening. So, I asked, "Are there any police in the next town?"

"You can use the telephone on the wall near the toilet," he said. "The police number is on the wall." Then as I began walking toward the phone, he added, "He won't thank you for phoning them."

The policeman identified his detachment and asked how he could help. Giving my name and describing where I was, I explained our situation.

To my surprise, he asked, "What do you want me to do about it?"

Taken aback for the second time, I adopted a problem-solving approach: "I want you to come and pick the fellow up and keep him from freezing to death."

In retrospect, things hadn't been going all that badly up until then. All I wanted was for the man lying on the road to have a good chance of surviving and for us to get home for Christmas.

"It's not our job," the policeman said.

And that is where I began to screw up. I blurted out, "Well, whose bloody job is it, anyway?"

It wasn't one of my better moments. I could have asked politely who I needed to contact, but I hadn't. In fact, I probably didn't think of it. Now, I had not only pissed off my boss in the truck, but I had also created a disgruntled policeman in the next town. The interview began to go by the numbers:

"What's your name again?"

"Where do you live?"

"Who do you work for?"

By this time, I might have been aware of the hole I was digging for myself, but any awareness I had didn't stop me from further digging, "I'll drop into the detachment on our way through and see if you have done anything."

Let's ignore the self-talk I was having at the time. I was frustrated, upset and not thinking all that well. Now, I was *in for a penny, in for a pound*, as the saying goes, and the policeman had hung up on me. The guy behind the counter in the café, who had heard most of it, was looking bemused and staying quiet. He had probably seen people out of control before.

My partner knew something was wrong the minute I got into the truck. I told him what had gone on with a growing feeling of regret.

He responded with "What an asshole."

He meant me.

He reluctantly agreed to drive slowly and see if the police went by us on our way out. They passed us a few minutes after we had driven by the man, who was still lying by the road.

The police car was moving very fast, and all its lights were flashing. There was a vast, rotating cloud of snow twisting into a long contrail behind them as they went by. We began to relax after we saw they weren't slowing to turn around and pull us over. Maybe, they were going too fast to see the decal on the side of our truck.

The rest of the trip home was a quiet one. My boss' anger appeared to slowly bleed off. We stayed calm when we drove past the police detachment, though I don't doubt both of us were thinking on the way by. We worked on a few more jobs together before I moved on, but we never did talk about that ride down the mountain. Occasionally, I wondered whether the man lying on the road survived. A stain began growing on my heart. It came because cultural differences made it difficult to intervene in his impending death. I thought about the police too. They did the right thing even though they were angry. But mostly, I thought of how little I knew about the situation they were all living in. And how I had made matters worse. As we were driving further and further from The Boss that day, I could still feel it there behind us. I can still feel it there today.

PRESENCE OF MIND

The water was dark with just a hint of deep, steely blueness carried under its surface. Small waves on top had a faint pinkish-orange colour on their edges. For a short while, they looked like penny arcade soldiers marching in cadence with the movement of the ferry we were on. It was a beautiful scene. One felt the waves, and the beauty that came from them might go on forever. But, of course, they couldn't last. A calm day would remove them, or they could hit a beach and break up. The break-up would be similar to my response when one of my deep breaths of the cool air around me caught a faint smell wafting across the strait from the Woodfibre pulp mill near Squamish. The first time I had smelled such an odour was on an earlier job. It had permeated our clothes and affected the taste of our food with an unnatural smell for days. I detected a hint of corruption riding with it in the air currents this time. My thoughts flew in every direction in what felt like an over-reaction, and I was no longer calm.

That first faint whiff of corruption had knocked me off the positive revery state induced by the beauty I had seen. The pulp mill represented the social and economic system we were living under. The pulp mill provided employment. It made some people rich, fed many of the rest of us, and even made the paper we wrote on. But now, it also poisoned us, as well as the nature around us. I began following a new line of thought induced by the smell.

My mind turned to the cold war between the United States and Russia. It was still going on in 1963 and a familiar topic. I was impressed by how propaganda from both sides contained lies of omission and commission. One social science student had even commented that the difference between our propaganda in the west and theirs was that ours was more effective. Perhaps the shock of the change I was experiencing wouldn't have been so severe if I didn't believe he was correct, and the pulp mill may not have become associated with lies in our own system. The pollution came from a technical problem, but the failure to deal with it was coming to look like a failure in our economic and political system. Indeed, one could rest there. But the mind is a tricky piece we all have, and, in a twist, mine went on to bring up Anton Chekhov.

Chekhov once told a story about a beautiful young woman. She belonged to a man who owned a mill and was so busy he didn't have time to wash. A young man watched the mill owner swimming in his mill pond one day. A circle of dirt spread around him as it passed from his body. The young man saw the young woman at the same time. The image of such beauty sleeping with someone carrying such dirt was disturbing. As you might guess, the young woman most likely represented Russia. Besmirching from the dirt was probably what Chekhov felt was being done to her by the system they were living under. For me, on that ferry, the smell from the pulp mill replaced Chekhov's dirt, and the beautiful woman being sullied became Canada.

I began wondering what Chekhov, who wrote before the Russian Revolution, would feel about the Russian soul if he was on the ferry with me now. The question fascinated me further when I considered reports of how senior members of the Communist Party were coming over to Johns Hopkins in the U.S. for medical care. At the very least, Chekhov would feel disappointed. You wouldn't find many of the proletariat at Johns Hopkins. They would be waiting on the streets for medical care back home.

As the ferry reached the pier, I was at the point of affirming that our beautiful woman still existed by claiming she distributed more wealth and didn't pollute as much as Russia. The bump from the ferry hitting the pier caused my thoughts to recede. I shook my whole body to throw off traces of revery and adopted a new mindset as we began moving toward the job site.

My workmate and I had been told that a boiler had exploded in the old powerhouse killing seven men. So, we went to have a look. Lord, how I hate those impulses to look. I don't intend to be disrespectful when they happen, but they diminish me just the same. Maybe we went because no one told us the men's names. Looking back, this seems to be important, but we didn't think about it then. For us, it was like the seven men hadn't existed until we saw the walls that were between us and where the boiler had been. They were made of reinforced cement at least one foot thick, maybe more. The section enclosing the boiler room had been reduced to rubble. The other one, which was closest to us, had holes blown in it a foot or two across. It was hard to comprehend the savagery of the blast.

We stood there paralyzed by what we were looking at. The seven men became real somehow, and the thought they didn't feel a thing was inescapable. How long does it take to feel pain? The enormous heat of the blast must have burned the blood they ejected. Thank God for that small mercy. Standing where we were, became a site of respect for lives lost, accompanied by a feeling of reverence. It stayed with us as we slowly began heading for the roof of the new powerhouse being built.

The roof was a busy place, with several trades working on it. A power tree was installed in its center for everyone to hook extensions into, and every outlet was being used. Luckily, we wouldn't need it ourselves. We could do any cutting and fitting by hand. Looking around, we saw the flashing we were to install already stacked on the roof. Somebody back in the office must have had a rare moment of clarity, and they had even coughed up for a crane! Seeing the pile smoothed out our day a bit. We had been dreading the job of getting the sheets up to the roof. Even using the lift would mean carrying the sheets individually. It would be tiring and take a lot of time. The flashing was big with a large face, and there was enough of it to do four sides of a big building. Our mood was elevated as we began installing.

My partner[8,] the sheet metal mechanic, had to hang over the edge of the roof while installing the sheets of flashing. As his helper, I did pretty much everything else; bring the piece over, hold it while he got a start positioning it, pass him tools and fasteners, and so on. The most challenging part of the job was listening to his bad jokes and sad stories about sex. I just saw all that as the norm and didn't take it seriously. Erotic fantasies aside, the mechanic had shown me several ways to improve my performance as a helper. Being indebted to him

---

[8] A feeling of partnership could develop in a journeyman/helper relationship. I had been on a number of jobs with this man, and he had taken my role as helper seriously. He would even give me hell for missing any mistakes he might be making. I liked him and felt a form of responsibility and loyalty toward him.

in this way, I found myself secretly training him to expect almost errorless performance. It had become somewhat of a game with us while on the job. For example, if my partner needed a hammer, I already had it there before he held his hand out. He would chide me if I didn't. I was now considering how to use his expectations to relieve some of the stress we had just been through.

Waiting between tool passes, while my boss was looking down and dealing with a tricky support bracket, I sat back and casually scanned the roof. My gaze became fixed on a man with a curiously humped stance. Just as I noticed him, he started shuffling rapidly toward the edge of the roof. His strange and dangerous behaviour shocked me into immobility. We were at least 50 feet up! Then, I saw one of the labourers working near me start running full-out toward the power tree. Diving onto it while clasping it to his chest, he began rotating his entire body and to pull out the plugs en masse as he fell toward the roof.

The guy who was shuffling dropped like a hanky about six feet from the edge. As fast as I have told you about it, everything was over. And I began coming out of my shock while starting to comprehend what had happened.

The shuffling man had shorted himself out on his circular saw. With his hands and arms frozen from the current going across his chest, he wasn't able to get rid of the saw that was hurting him. So, he began running away. The labourer, realizing what was happening and knowing at that instant that he didn't have time to look for an individual plug, did the only thing that could work in the time the rest of us sat staring. It took an incredibly well-prepared state of mind to do what he had. I could only view his feat in wonderment.

We all remained in place while another worker did artificial respiration to the man lying on the roof. Soon, the man's breathing came back, and someone helped him sit up. Nothing more could be done. The rest of us went back to work as one of the workers supported the man to the first aid shack.

After the event, it took me a while to get my mechanic back into his expectant mode of operating. Once he was running well, I waited until the last sheet before handing him a screwdriver instead of the hammer he was expecting. The screwdriver had a nice big handle on it. I figured that thickness, along with his expectations, would briefly stop him from knowing it wasn't a hammer. All that would be needed was a few seconds, especially reaching back for it while lying on his belly the way he was. He had had a lot of time by then to get used to errorless performance. The plan worked perfectly! When I handed him the screwdriver handle instead of the hammer, he hit the clip with it. He was even raising the screwdriver to hit the clip again, before stopping to see why it hadn't worked so well. Then holding the screwdriver in front of his face, he rolled over on his back. I can still see him lying there on the roof with his hand in front of his face, gazing at the screwdriver. He was laughing so hard he was almost crying. God bless the proletariat, our lives were beautiful again, and we were happy in our state.

VIMY RIDGE DAY

The old Lie
Dulce et decorum est
Pro patria mori
– Wilfred Owen

The journey to a final Vimy Ridge Day began with hearing my grampa crying at night. I was very young, and I remember my mother and grandmother, who came to check on me that night, telling me not to be frightened. They said the steel[9] he was carrying in his leg from WWI made him cry out. Maybe it was hearing his cries that made me remember the things he told my father about *the war to end all wars*. I only remembered fragments of what grampa said. All I could hear of my father talking was a background murmur. He told me what the vestiges of memories meant years later when I asked him about them. What I heard as a child, was the beginning of a torturous path stretching through many experiences, over many years. The end of the path would happen on our final Vimy Ridge Day. But the place to start is with what Grampa said to my dad.

The statements I recall him making are in quotes. What my father told me, and what I believe they probably meant, follows the quotes. I took father's interpretations for my own.

> "A band would march down the street and the young men would come out in droves to sign up."

Grampa was saying all it took for the young men to be recruited for WWI was a band marching down the street. He wasn't being critical of the young men. But he felt they had no understanding of

---

[9] Grampa was shot. Bullets used in the war were said to be jacketed with steel. There were also jackets made of different metals. The steel ones were intended to pierce armour. So, the language used may be loose here. There was also an idea that jacketed bullets would wound, rather than kill. Wounding a soldier caused greater pressure on economic and other social systems supporting the other side.

the horror that would follow.

"There were bodies every few feet on Westminster bridge."

People had a lot of sex in England during WWI, some of it took place on Westminster bridge. He wasn't talking about corpses.

"They should have left the poor bastards alone."

He was talking about the abuse of two homosexual men in the army.

"I saw her laying under a bush! Some bastard had killed her!"

Grampa was telling Dad about a little girl he had seen while in France. He saw her crying and looking for her parents earlier in the day. She was murdered later and stuffed under a bush. (As far as I can recall, this was my first intimation that there were casualties other than soldiers.)

"We could hear the priests blessing the Germans in their trenches. We could hear them singing Christmas carols like us too."

Probably they were talking about why Grampa came back an atheist. It sounded like he saw the German soldiers as humans in the same mess he was.

"The poor bloody horses were the worst."

Grampa was talking about the corpses of the horses that pulled the caissons. He could still smell them rotting. It feels significant to me that the deaths of the horses were what bothered him the most. It was probably their innocence that made him feel that way.

My father told me that Grampa was a man who lost all his companions while fighting in the trenches during WWI. He lost his friends within 15 feet of the top they went over during their first battle. They ran into machine-gun fire without artillery support. The attack had been called off and the messenger who was riding a bike to the front was killed. So, they had to follow orders and go over the top without artillery support. Grampa was shot in his leg but got up and ran toward the back lines when he saw the German mop-up squads come out and go to work. I can still see him showing my father how it was done. The soldier would approach the body on the ground sticking his bayonet into it while it was before him. Continuing to walk by the dead soldier while dragging his rifle, the bayonet would come out of the body. Sometimes it would stick, and the soldier would have to pull on the rifle to get it out.

> "They found his pistol unfired surrounded by the bodies of his patrol."

Grampa was telling a story about Winston Churchill's participation in a previous war, probably the Boer War. He was a bit of an expert on Churchill's life. As with religion, he had no use for politicians when he returned from WWI. His view toward them was very negative, including Churchill, despite the glorification of the latter's role by desperate people during WWII. I'm pretty sure it was because he believed politicians didn't go to war themselves or copped out if they did. There is little doubt, however, his view was broader than just the role of politicians. He felt war was one of life's failures, and governments, industry, and religions were primarily responsible for it. He had no use for medals either, feeling they were often given out arbitrarily.

The cumulative impression left to me by these early memories about war was one of betrayal of honest, hardworking folk by the organizations influencing their lives. After those early years, my attitude toward war laid pretty fallow for a long time. It did so even during the Korean war outbreak in 1950. My mind was still busy beneath it all, but it was usually concerned about other things.

An awakening began in a logging camp when I was about 18 years old. There was a sad, blocky little man in the camp. He could work and had found his place, I suppose. But I couldn't like him. The feeling was a visceral one. Things became clearer to me one day when we were all in the bunkhouse, and he started talking about WWII and the liberation of Holland. His most significant memory about the liberation was how he could go into a house and crawl into bed with a young female and have sex with her. Becoming visibly excited, he described how warm they were and how great it all was. To the rest of us, who were ominously silent, it was a skin-crawling thing. We were all linked in our feelings in some way that I didn't fully understand and probably never will. For at that moment, we had been confronted by something unacceptably ambivalent. It would be nice to have sex with a warm young woman in a soft bed, especially in our deprived state. But there was something wrong with the man and how he talked.

The man was entirely re-living the experience before us while telling us about it, and there was no doubt he was aroused. He was a bit simpleminded, but not so simple he didn't know what rape was. He didn't appear to care about the women at all.

Did his talk reveal a part of nature in all of us? Was love born in rape? Were all men potential rapists? Some of the more extreme feminists said so during later years. Their thoughts included my much-loved father and grampa. Are all women potential whores? Be careful; the thought includes my much-loved mother and grandmothers! My desire to kill the sick, simple bastard was backed by all the hormones in a young male. It was based on a revulsion as violent and powerful as any I've experienced without acting on it. I can only speculate about why it didn't happen. He may not have done what he did until war provided the impetus and a safe venue to do it in. But he was stuck there, and the putrid smell of war grew larger in me seeing it.

Let's avoid the phony comfort of further rational analysis. My reaction was emotional and may not bear any relationship to reason. At that time, I believed that war was something the men who had paid their dues didn't talk about. When they did speak of it, they didn't revel in it or glorify it. The topic was spoken in quiet tones with periods of silence between them.

I re-visited the liberation of Holland many years later with another man. He was imprisoned by the war too, but his heart was good, and so was his head. As is the case in many male friendships, we met and came to know each other through physical activity, tai chi, in this instance. We did talk but rarely talked about the war, and then only in abstract terms. It hadn't occurred to me that he had served during WWII when I told him about a war movie. One part of the movie was about an American General who commanded a strategic tank battle against the Germans. At one point, I mentioned that the American tanks ran on gas and were prone to burning easily, going on to extoll the virtues of the German 88 and diesel, which burned with more difficulty. My friend confirmed the difference in fuels and the viability of the 88. Continuing, he said that he had arrived at similar conclusions while serving in the tank corps during WWII. It startled me at the time. But the conversation didn't go much further, and I didn't think about it much more. Then, one day he mentioned that the Dutch had invited all the vets who had participated in the liberation of Holland during WWII to come to a celebration.

I hadn't thought about my friend having been in Holland with his tank when we talked about the movie. When I asked him if he would go, he replied that he didn't know. Liking him and not wondering why he was hesitating, I tried to encourage him. Not wanting to hurt his pride, I joked a bit by telling him that I had some money for the trip if he was broke. He was quite proud in his quiet way, and one can't be entirely sure what is going on with people. My friend didn't appear to be particularly upset; he even grinned. Thanking me for the offer, he assured me he didn't need my money.

It was only when we were having lunch one day after my friend came back that I began to wonder what he was experiencing. When I asked him about the trip, he told me of the positive events the Dutch held for the vets and how well everyone had treated them. It was only as he was describing the grand march down the streets, with the vets wearing their service medals and the Dutch people lining the streets cheering them, that he began to cry. Not knowing what to do, I got up and went to get us another coffee. After returning with the coffee, I just sat there and let him cry.

A beast was sitting unacknowledged beside us when he stopped, but we didn't talk "about it. I think we were both hoping it would go away. I never did get up the nerve to ask him about it, and the topic didn't come up again between us. I just hoped he was OK. Isn't it curious that, while writing about the event and my friend's crying after talking about Holland, I managed to join it to my experience with the man in that logging camp? I hadn't truly appreciated the impact of my friend knowing the things that went on during the liberation. He's gone now, and I can't ask him. Maybe it's just as well. In his way, he told me. I should be able to take it from there.

Two other experiences were in the background while sitting at lunch with my friend that day. Neither involved Holland in any obvious way, but they were important just the same. I was installing metal faces and doors on the entrances to the chutes in a rehabilitation hospital when the first experience happened. The work site was near the main aisles on each floor, and I could see people passing by all the time. Looking down the hall, I saw an old fellow come out of a door near the end and start slowly shuffling toward where I was working. He was dressed in a blue hospital smock of some kind. The old fellow was still trucking but clearly wasn't in the company notch, as I might have said at the time. It took him until 10:00 a.m. and my coffee break to arrive at the fire doors just past where I was working—I had come in and began working at 8:00 a.m. The doors were wide enough to allow passage of hospital beds and gurneys two-abreast. They were hung on narrow walls projecting from the main walls. The hospital kept the doors open. I was told they only closed them during a fire. The old fellow had been moving in a straight line until arriving near the doors. While watching him and drinking my coffee, I figured he would pass through them easily. Instead of preserving his straight-line shuffle, however, the man developed a sharp curve to the right and stopped in the corner made by the door and the wall. It was pure slow-motion slapstick, and I even chuckled to myself a bit. Instead of coming back out of the corner though, he just continued standing there for the duration of my coffee break. Many people were moving up and down the hall, but they all went by him without stopping to help. My humorous mood began changing to something more negative.

Finally, feeling critical about what was happening, I downed tools. Walking over to help him and reaching out to grab him, I was stopped by someone grabbing my arm from behind.

"Don't!" a voice said.

Annoyed at being grabbed, I turned and saw an orderly of some kind holding my arm.

"Why?" I asked him, my annoyance undiminished.

"Because I don't want him to quit," he said. "Once he quits, he won't start up again!"

The orderly wanted the old fellow to get out of the corner on his own, which eventually he was able to do. I had been too judgmental and in too much of a hurry to help. It occurred to me that all those in hospital uniforms who had been passing by without helping would know this. Chastened, I apologized and told him that I didn't understand what was happening. After confessing my ignorance, I asked the orderly about a room down the hall from us. People had been going in and out of the room while I was working. One person was a priest, and I was pretty sure another was a minister. I had also seen a group of middle-aged women I thought were a PTA group, who went in the day before, too. Those were the only people I saw visiting, apart from an orderly or nurse, despite having been around for visiting hours the night before.

"Oh!" the orderly said. "That's where the WWI vets are! There are seven of them left. They don't have any arms and legs and are kept in baskets."

When he told me who was there, I felt that I should go into the room and say hello, maybe even see if I could help somehow. But emotional cowardice kept me from that room. I was afraid I wouldn't know what to say or do. I felt ashamed of it then, and I still do. I felt aggressive and defensive about it and want to tell the truth about the matter. It's time to go to the east coast of Canada for the other experience before we return to the west for my final Vimy Ridge Day and the man and resolution I met there.

While I would eventually come to see the beauty of the Maritimes, living in Dartmouth during the winter was one of the grimmer times of my life. Each morning going down Albro Lake Road, I would catch the bus and go to the university where I was studying. The wind off Bedford Basin cut like a knife. It went completely through my clothing. I don't believe I have experienced such a cutting wind since. The apartment complex my wife and I were living in provided little sanctuary. It conducted sounds as efficiently as copper wire conducts electric current. It even seemed to amplify them. The worst noise came from the young people next door to us, who had a crying baby. The husband kept slamming the crib against a wall each night while shouting at the baby to stop crying. It upset us so much we couldn't sleep. After a few nights of desperation, I went to their door and pounded on it while loudly asking if they were OK. Things went silent after that, but we continued to have trouble sleeping, and our unhappiness remained. The silence was bothersome too. The setting was admirably suited to prepare me for the experience I had on the bus.

It was quiet and dark outside when I came home exhausted around 10:00 p.m. one night. The streetlights were a dark orange colour. Not providing much illumination, they seemed to be sucking energy from their surroundings. The dimness outside was echoed inside the bus, where the lights had a similar orange tinge. The air was warm in the bus, but, somehow, its mugginess made the warmth oppressive. All in all, the conditions provided a perfect accompaniment to the depression and fatigue I was feeling. The only other person on the bus was a man sitting in the seat across from me. He was an older man with a solid, non-threatening aspect, suggesting he was just another person alone on a bus, like me.

I'm not sure how it was that we ended up talking about war. I think it was the outlines of warships we could both see in the basin below us as we travelled across the bridge to Dartmouth. The scene led to my mentioning the mistreatment of the British merchant marine during WWII. There was a section about them in a book I was reading about the Murmansk Run written by Alistair MacLean. (I read detective and adventure stories for relief from the demands of the other kind of reading I was doing.) I recall telling my fellow Traveler how the book said that people could only last about 30 minutes in the water when their ship was sunk on that run.

The other passenger, possibly realizing I didn't know whether to believe the fact and feeling he should be polite, replied, "You know, some guys put their life jackets on backward because of that."

My God, he had been there! He had been on convoys travelling the Murmansk Run. Not knowing why men would put their life jackets on backward, I asked him why they did it.

"It was because, if they had to jump off the ship," he said, "the jacket would break their neck when they hit the water. Death was so certain they didn't want to prolong the experience."

It's a measure of the state we were both in that there was nothing remarkable about this. He had stated a fact, and I had accepted it.

Vimy Ridge Day was when Grampa met those remaining in his regiment each year. I can still see my dad, uncle, and me standing on the lawn, talking quietly and waiting to take him with us. The meeting was held in a room downstairs in a café in a dingier part of town. The staff treated us respectfully, as was usual. They hung national and regimental flags behind our table. We had the normal social period, then were called to sing the national anthem and make toasts to the queen and regiment. A member called the roll. This time, there were seven men left in his regiment. My memory resonated at the number seven. It was the number of men in the baskets at that hospital. I felt shame and sadness again.

Letters and telegrams from those that couldn't make it to the meeting were read, which was appreciated by the those present. We stood for two minutes' silence, lest we forget. After that, we had lunch, followed by more socializing before going home. The social period was when Grampa would sometimes drink too much. Vimy Ridge Day was the only time I ever saw him drink like that. He didn't drink much this time, and we got him home safely afterward, as usual. The three of us did not say much during the drive. I don't know about the others, but I had more to think about on that drive home than ever before.

This particular Vimy Ridge Day had been like the previous ones in most ways, but there were some differences. Draft dodgers were coming up from the U.S. into Canada during the war in Vietnam. Like many other Canadians, I wasn't sure what to think about them. Would they be willing to fight to protect our country? The apposition of numbers from those remaining in the regiment, and the number of the men I knew might still be in baskets in the hospital, had also upset me. I had found out they were all dead, and felt sad, ashamed, and relieved all at the same time. There are chances that go away and when they do, you can't get them back.

During lunch, on this Vimy Ridge Day, I had sat beside a man who had been through a gas attack. I had noticed the sound of his breathing while eating lunch. At first, I hadn't understood what I was hearing or where it came from. The memory of it is so fresh that I could mimic it. Realizing it was coming from the man beside me,

I looked and saw him holding his face close to his soup and slowly sliding each spoonful past his breathing. Seeing him, I began the final leg of my journey. Somehow, the vet being so compromised made the draft dodgers coming into Canada pop into my mind. Would I, as a young man, be brave enough to fight? Should I go? I wasn't even brave enough to see the fortune dished out by war at that hospital. I sat there confused while sneaking fearful looks at the old fellow suffering the results of a gas attack. The sight of him and the sounds he was making were terrible!

God help me! I blurted out my big question: "What do you think of the draft dodgers coming up from the States?"

The old fellow didn't say anything, though he must have heard the question about the draft dodgers because his spoon stopped moving, though he kept his face close to his soup. My neck became hot and my guts started twisting. Had I mentioned something that shouldn't be talked about? He remained sitting there with his face above his soup, and his silence seemed to go on forever. I wanted to run but remained frozen in my seat. I had nowhere to go, except out to the car and wait for my companions. If I did that, my fear and embarrassment would be visible for all to see. So, I continued sitting there not knowing what to do.

Finally, turning his head above his soup and looking me right in the eyes, the old vet said, in his breathing-challenged voice, "Fuck-em! I wouldn't go!"

HORST

Getting off the train, I saw a beagle innocently sniffing around a telephone pole before it trotted into the street. Who knows what was on its mind? Certainly, the poor driver didn't. Seeing the car trying to stop, the beagle began running back to the side of the street. But the nearest front tire of the car went over it, leaving it underneath the chassis baying pitifully. Only a most hardened person wouldn't have felt sorry for that poor dog. I tried comforting myself with the thought that the beagle had a chance of surviving. They are a toughly knit breed, and there was that mournful sound it was making to encourage the idea. At least it could make a sound.

Such an accident was a poor beginning for someone who had travelled 4500 miles to a strange place to pursue an advanced degree. Looking back, I can see that what happened to the beagle foreshadowed what would happen to me. Coming from a happy and productive lab, I had now landed in one that was unhappy and not productive. In other words, I had landed in the soup. Looking back, I see myself as somewhat similar to bees or other insects that have made a mistake and keep swimming around on the water they have landed in, unable to escape. I'm not sure they would feel the isolation I was feeling after arriving at the university, but they certainly did appear to emulate my developing defensiveness.[10] The intensity of my feelings took me by surprise. They made it hard for me to think and undoubtedly influenced how I acted around Horst. He was one of the unusual people I met there. And, as far as I could see, he was removed from the conflict that was going on, though he must have been aware of it. How could he not?

---

[10] The situation was complicated. There were significant political and intellectual arguments going on in the department. They related to questions of legitimate areas for study in psychology and even to the issue of how to test doctoral candidates. Such arguments can be quite vicious in academe, though I didn't know it before landing where I did. My lab mates were friendly, but they were on the outs with the powers that be in the department and were unhappy.

Horst was a deceptively unassuming man. It wasn't until one experienced him on his chosen path that his intelligence, courage, dedication, and fierceness would come to the fore. His interest was biological science and research in all its forms, and he was passionate about it. He was so knowledgeable that I eventually coined the term; 'comparative everthingus' in my head when describing him to myself. It was a wry, respectful description that developed while seeing how broad his studies were. My fellow graduate students had told me of his dedication before I met him and had impressed upon me that his favourite subject was fish. They said he could turn any topic in the direction of his finny friends. And they recounted brief stories concerning how Horst had gone to God-awful places to study eels and their relationship with the moon. He took time to study bats along the way, too.

I knew little of Horst's personal life, and I didn't work with him directly on a project. My exposure to him, while memorable, was episodic. He worked in a lab down the hall from me, usually out of sight. His limited exposure made me curious about him. I even recall wondering what his wife, whom I had never met, was like. The idea popped into my head that she must be like Mrs. Pavlov; that poor beleaguered woman, married to the dual Nobel Laureate, Mr. Pavlov. I was told that she had to help him find any train he wished to travel on. One wag even said that she had to hold his hand while he was getting on board to prevent him from wandering off.

While having some intangible truth to it, this speculation was unfair to Horst and probably his wife as well. Horst could find more difficult things than a train and could survive hazardous circumstances while doing so. As for his wife, she was reported to have hardly turned a hair after being told that he had disappeared from the department. Nevertheless, I still saw a similarity between them and the Pavlovs, however misplaced.

Fish and Me in Warm Water

The first time I saw Horst was when he entered the coffee room one morning. I had just finished reading an article in the local rag concerning a heavy water plant raising the water temperature in the local ocean basin. No doubt designed to cause some ire in its readers, the article was strident and apocalyptic. The paper prophesizing that the change would kill fish made me think that bringing it up with Horst would be a good way of meeting him. It was at this point that the defensiveness I mentioned earlier cut in. I was on tenterhooks while approaching him, fearing he would find the article trivial. My memory of the meeting contains only impressions accompanied by a few facts. There is little doubt that my unbalanced state would be evident to him. I cringe while looking back, though I probably did manage to describe at least some of the article.

Horst's reaction was underwhelming. I still believe he may even have been acting in a minor way to calm me down, though I felt he was sincere. After looking at me, he continued a slow walk over to the coffee urn and poured a cup of coffee.

Turning back, while adopting a thoughtful look, he said

I was concerned that science had resulted in the use of nuclear energy to kill people in Japan. Then, there was our failure to feed everyone despite having many Nobel laureates in economics, and the progress biological science had provided in agriculture, to rely on. Horst's dedication to research would become abundantly clear later on. But circumstances never seemed to arise when I would get a chance to ask him where he placed science in relation to social issues. Would he favour or reject scientism, for example? Would he accept that science created social problems in addition to helping solve them? Are we creating so many problems by relying on science and technology that we are hastening our demise as a species? How I wish I was at the stage where I could have asked him about such issues.

The Fish in the Tank

Horst's lessons, while far-reaching, weren't always mild.

Seeing him working in his lab with the door open one day, I impulsively blazed in and called to him, "Hey, Horst. What do you think of Konorski's theoretical model concerning the neural basis for learning?"

Continuing to describe a publication on the topic I had just read and why I found it so fascinating, I must have been ignoring his reaction. It impressed me as much as the article I had read, though in an unexpected way. It wasn't so much that Horst introduced me to Siamese fighting fish. Who could be surprised by that? It's a fish, and I was dealing with Horst. What was remarkable was how he did the introduction.

With my enthusiasm in full flight, it took me some time to see he wasn't impressed by what I was saying.

The light began to dawn when he grabbed my arm in a vice-like grip and began dragging me across his lab, loudly repeating, "You see that! That's real! You see that! That's real!"

Looking around frantically while trying to prevent my shoulder from being dislocated, all I could see was a fish tank across the lab from us—nothing new there. What the hell was he talking about? As we continued our collision course toward the tank, it became apparent that Horst was pointing at a fish. The feeling of comfort with a favourite topic emerged in me. It was a Siamese fighting fish and a female, at that. Frankly, the fish didn't look like such a big deal. If we were fishing, we would have had to throw it back or use it for bait to catch bigger fish. So, a bit chuffed about being dragged around by my arm, I asked him what was so special about it.

Making a magnificent effort to calm down while slightly relaxing his grip, Horst continued toward the tank, dragging me with him until we stood close enough to see the fish. Explaining that he was pointing at the red streak on its side, he asked if I could see it. Receiving a cautious and suspicious, "yes," from me, he went on to say, "The initial response by the male to the female during courtship is a homicidal sequence that changes to one of lovemaking when she flashes the magic red streak on her side". A tiny red line seemed to be a pretty small thing to hinge one's personal survival on. (It appears that mother nature can do such things, and there is peril associated with not paying attention to her.)

I would have liked to know how Horst applied this knowledge to the relationship between human males and females. Having been lucky in getting off with just a stiff shoulder, however, I was reluctant to ask. We didn't appear to be in an appropriate situation for the irreverent humour I went in for, and the relationship probably wouldn't be a direct one. Today, I wish I had asked. Lord only knows what Horst would have said. It would most likely have been interesting and informative. Sadly, it will have to remain as another example of an opportunity lost.

Reflecting on Horst's actions that day, I realized he reinforced the importance of basing one's thinking on verifiable facts. That red stripe, and the immediate change made by the male fish upon seeing it, were things that we could agree about. Indeed, we must agree about them. Perhaps Horst was also saying that one should see a physically tangible thing and get on with the job of describing the mechanisms behind it rather than talking about some fictional process like learning.

Where the problem lay for me in Horst's reaction was that the things I was interested in, like cognition, perception, and learning, weren't directly observable. When is the last time you saw or weighed a kilogram of mind, for example? I was pretty sure Horst wasn't against theories, either. So, what followed for me after the Siamese fighting fish episode was some confusion accompanied by having imaginary debates with him in my mind. It's always easier to be intellectually brave in one's own head.

There are so many questions I could have asked Horst. Do we create reality? I think we do. Is there a physical universe we can study? I believe there is. Do you have to experience things directly for them to be real? Damn it, Horst. I don't think we do. We can do so by seeing their effect. So, is the mind real? Yup. Is God real? Yes, God is real in all its, his, or her manifestations because human creations have consequences. We create them, and they are as real as any observable physical entity. Is God dead? Only to the people who believe they, or it, or an inanimate object is. (I have one friend who talks to rocks.) OK, if we create intangible things, how do we do it? We think them up. Is it a matter of 'faith?' Of course, it is, and probably repetition and seeing the consequences of our beliefs. Faith is real, too. We created it.

Finally, I decided we create things when we don't have a god or nature to do it for us. I still wouldn't walk blindly into an intersection, believing a Mack truck would fail to smear me all over the road if I just believed hard enough. But, circular, or not, ill-advised, or not, somehow the beliefs got me through. Horst might not agree with any of these answers, you understand. He did like to say there was nothing new under the sun.

Meanwhile, physicists, who may be our last hope, and who have become very good at manipulating tiny and intangible things in the domain they work in, appear to be banking on building a quantum computer to tell us something about the mind. Some even say the mind might not reside in our heads but is distributed throughout the universe. For me, these facts provide some compensation. A large number of much brighter people are as confused as I am. Gee, thanks Horst; here we are waiting for the physicists to do something again. I keep wondering what our minds will do with that quantum computer if physicists are successful in building one. Early attempts to replicate the mind with direct electrical stimulation of the brain suggested that it was always located one neuron over. "That was you, not me," it said. Things are going to get interesting if they build that computer.[11]

Cutting Fish Retina

A questionable side benefit of the fish-tank incident, apart from my philosophical confusion, was that it allowed Horst to reverse our roles. The reversal had a strange beginning. One day he passed below the red light that hung over the door of my lab workspace while talking to himself. The red light, as you no doubt know, is a universal symbol that other people are busy and don't wish to be disturbed. He was either confused while wandering in talking to himself, or he needed to bounce his musing off someone else and anyone would do. I suppressed any animosity I felt for the invasion and assumed the role of anybody. After all, he probably had to extend the same consideration to me during the Siamese fishing lesson. Nevertheless,

---

[11] Wilder Penfield was stimulating the brains in patients with epilepsy back then. He found that he could trigger concrete actions, even memories but never abstract thought. His patients could always tell when Penfield triggered something and when they did so themselves. Despite reviewing many thousands of epileptic events, Penfield never found an epileptic seizure involving thoughts. Much has been written on the mind/body problem. There is a podcast in which Michael Egnor talks about this topic for those who are interested. (Michael Egnor: Is There Evidence for a Soul? Mindmatters.ai/podcast/ep70/2020)

I soon found it difficult standing there while having no idea what he was talking about. Just as I began wondering if I should grab his arm and begin dragging him around the lab as he had me, he mentioned fish—*no surprise there*—the retina— *some surprise there*. The man was an elemental force in pursuit of such topics, and probably couldn't be disrupted anyway. So, I remained mute while trying to put clues together concerning what he was talking about. Continuing to nod at the right times was an uphill battle, and all I was able to do was hear a few more technical terms. 'Embedding compound and Sections[12]' were two, and they were somehow related to the fish retinas he mentioned. I hadn't been quite successful in understanding what was going on when Horst suddenly stopped talking. Looking confused for a moment, he then turned around and passed back under the red light going the other way. He didn't say hello and he didn't say goodbye, as they say. I felt I had come out of the situation rather well having survived, but my interest was now aroused, and it hadn't been satisfied.

Running into other beleaguered graduate students the next day provided me with an opportunity to gather more information. The students were discussing a demonstration by Horst in his lab showing how he could polish the tip of a glass micro-electrode pipette using his finger. As I recall, the tip of the pipette is several microns in diameter. They believed it was impossible, but were coming around to Horst's view after using very strong magnification to test his claim in an impromptu blind study. It was nice to talk to people who were as confused by him as I was. Appearing grateful to change the topic under discussion, they began filling me in about what was concerning Horst when he had waltzed into my lab space.

After his monologue, Horst went back to his lab, having decided he must repeat an experiment from its very beginning. He had raised fish in different visual environments to study the development of their visual systems. Two of the environments contained only horizontal or vertical contours on the walls of the tanks the fish were housed in. While analyzing his results, he noticed that he hadn't standardized the position of each fish retina in its embedding compound. Not

---

[12] Embedding compound was a substance used to hold delicate things together while they were sliced into very thin sections using a microtome.

standardizing the position of the retinas meant that the sections (slices) would be cut at slightly different angles. The whole debate with himself, concerned whether Horst could legitimately use the thinnest section from each preparation for making comparisons between the groups he was studying. Deciding he couldn't and would have to repeat the entire experiment, meant months of work would go down the drain, let alone thousands of dollars.

The decision to redo the experiment would probably have caused Horst considerable personal pain. In fact, in similar circumstances, many would be tempted to cheat. After all, who would know, or be able to prove it; if one lied by omission? The argument for using the thinnest section from each retina for comparison purposes is certainly logical and could even be correct. If it provided a correct answer, others would get similar results, and everything would be OK. If using the preparations proved to be the wrong thing to do, other researchers would get a different result. There were a number of possibilities in the situation, but the central issue is that others being able to replicate someone else's results is a fundamental requirement in science. Lying about it is wrong. Failures to replicate can be very hard to track down. The researcher who couldn't replicate a result would also be expected to provide a reason for the failure. Failure to do so would suggest there was an uncontrolled, unknown variable floating around.

It's only human to be tempted to cheat, but misrepresentation wasn't Horst's way. His personal integrity and concern for standards in scientific inquiry won out, and he repeated his studies. He was a man who wrote his errors in red. Others in the department were capable of such integrity, and I saw them make similar decisions. They might make errors or mistakes, but their behaviour commanded respect, and, seeing them do what they did, I resolved to do the same. Horst's actions also confirmed for me that emotion was equally as important as rational thought, if not more so.

Regardless of how creative rationalizations were; reason, logic, and fact, that didn't 'feel' right to me, no longer determined my final view. I didn't reject reasoned discussion or argument. Indeed, I might hold such as my view. But the fact so much of our brain has evolved to be concerned with emotions supported, for me, the idea, that one should hold reason accountable to feelings. The view I adopted has helped me keep going in situations where reason led to what I 'felt' were incorrect conclusions, reprehensible ends, or immoral acts.

While I was putting emotion in an important, even ascendant position, in relation to reason, I was also becoming responsible for my own thinking. It's a lonely place to be. When it happens, you can feel naked. Your thinking can diverge from all others around you. It can be entirely wrong, and you can no longer act like a coward and blame others for it. It's a world in which our personal uniqueness is what we have to offer, and it underlies the contribution you and I make. The world I was entering demanded we say what we believed without artifice or obfuscation. If you, or anyone else, regardless of the medium of exchange, told me something, I was responsible for accepting or rejecting it, as well as for where I went with it from then on. No wonder Horst struggled so hard to protect his research, and I was struggling so hard to protect my own thoughts.

The Electrical Static Invasion

The distance Horst was willing to go to in protecting his research was apparent in other instances. One such instance occurred in relation to the construction of the new Life Sciences Complex the university was building at the time. It is hard to imagine the amount of work involved in the planning and execution of such a project. The size of the job alone makes it likely that there will be some errors along the way.

There had been many faculty meetings to review planning and minimize such errors. The meeting of present concern occurred near the end of construction when the plan for covering the floors in our wing was being presented. Graduate students were invited, so I was present when Horst noticed the floors were to be carpeted. He pointed out in a forthright manner what an error this would be. His quiet and lucid presentation was much like the brief period of stillness that precedes some change in weather. It seemed clear, to me, that others should heed what he was saying.

Horst's concern was a dire one from the perspective of his research, and ours. Many of us were doing sensitive electrical recordings that involved very small signals. Carpeted floors would generate electrical static and disrupt them. The problem seemed obvious to me at the time and still does. To this day, I don't know what led to Horst's opinion being ignored. The floors ended up covered with carpet. I suppose it is possible some people are attracted to a colour resembling that of a bad case of diarrhea, but that was only the beginning of the problem. Predictably, static electricity Travelled right along with the bilious colour.

I came in early the day after the carpeting had been installed. Horst had come in even earlier. Standing in the hallway in his gumboots, he looked magnificent. Having unspooled the wall-mounted fire hose, which he had going full-bore, he was soaking our entire floor. The water would eliminate the static, you see, and it did. Sadly, I didn't hear the discussions that must have happened between the various powers-that-be concerning the flooding. I'm sure those discussions would have been delightful for some and nauseating for others. But I did see the same crew that installed the carpeting come back to remove it. They looked resigned. Life continued, with static-free recording.

The Impromptu Trip

One day, Horst disappeared from the department. It took a couple of days for people to realize he was gone. Concern grew while members of the department were looking for him. It was quickly established that no one knew where he was. When approached, Horst's wife reportedly indicated she didn't know, either. She only appeared mildly concerned about it, according to some, which gave them the impression that such a disappearance wasn't unusual.

But the hunt was on by that time. Horst was finally found to have taken a flight to Philadelphia, where he visited the Museum of Natural History during off-hours. It was quite a feat tracing him that far. I was told that the only clue departmental members had was a book on his desk opened to a picture of a photographic plate showing a fish. The plate was known to be stored at the museum, and Horst wanted to look at the plate. Apparently, he felt the fish shown on it was a transitional form between two separate species, and he wanted to have a closer look.

Letting Horst into the museum after closing hours, the curator, obviously aware of who (or what) he was dealing with, watched him happily examining the photographic plate. He also watched him leaving in the middle of the night. It seems Horst, becoming convinced the plate showed a fish that was the transition stage he expected, went off to the Amazon. Having seen similar fish while studying eels there, apparently, he knew where to look.

The department's search stalled at the point of his departure from the museum. Time passed until the search was ended by a phone call coming from a hospital in South America telling the department that Horst was under their care.

Apparently, our hero had staggered out of the Amazon jungle onto what passed for a road while carrying a plastic bag containing some fish. A weekly bus arrived at the scene on the day Horst had collapsed there. Luckily, he was able to give instructions about how to care for the fish before passing out.

I have a picture in my mind of Horst lying on the road with his arm valiantly pointing up to the bag of water with his fish in it on top of the bus, instructing the driver about how to care for them. Horst survived his stay in the hospital. The result of his adventure was two new fish and a transitional form.

My Journey Ends

The last time I saw Horst, he told me I had passed my final essay. He said it was the worst he had ever read, but went on to say, "What could I do? It was your Ph.D."

He was right. I had gone from writing an essay my first committee had said was very good indeed, to the worst which Horst claimed he had ever seen. The topic was in an area I had already published in, too. So, I left for a couple of years and went teaching.

After a phone call from the Dean of Graduate Studies in which he asked, "Fred are you ever going to finish this degree you started?" I went back and finished. It seemed to be a small victory for a few of us, and I am glad of that. But, somewhere in that time of going back to finish, I had lost track of Horst, and never saw him again.

Where is Horst Now?

Many years have gone by since I was where we were at that time. I wasn't in touch with Horst much while I was there, and I was even further away after leaving. Realizing the personal importance of what I experienced, and writing this story, I feel like thanking him. The feeling is a true one; and feeling and truth count. I see Horst in some wild place where there is something finny to observe. Or maybe he just left his bones there. We are all older now, and leaving bones seems more likely. If it's true of Horst, the creator's blessing be upon him: a wild place would be one where he could belong. If he is in a place that is more restricted, I hope it will allow for finny friends, even if they are only in a glass bowl rather than a tank. Will he choose one with a red stripe on its side? I hope he does and chooses one without a stripe, as well. It would be good if there are some students to visit him who are smart enough to recognize the 'real deal,' when confronted by it. I would have liked to have been able to thank him, as well as some others there. I'd tell him I did my best to live up to their example, even though it took me time to find another road. Maybe that act of thanking would surprise him as his Siamese fighting fish lesson surprised me.

NIGHT LESSONS

It had been a hard day and was looking to be a hard night. Lord only knew what time it was, probably around 10 p.m. The day had begun with an observation that some of the motor seizures I was studying started differently from others. Until then, I thought they all had the same beginning. After analyzing videotapes until my eyes felt like they were dropping out onto my cheeks, it became clear the motor seizures that began differently were suppressed completely only to reappear with the same beginning all the others had. Sure enough, there was a regression phase in the development of some seizures.

Hmmm, I thought. *They had to go back and get it right!*

That was about as far as my thinking went on the subject. With a wave of exhaustion sweeping through a mind turning in circles, I turned off the equipment and went to lie down in the solarium. One day, my advisor would say that we both understood the importance of the observation while suggesting that I leave the 30 pages I had written about it out of my thesis. He believed my advisory committee wouldn't have the same understanding. But what I had seen remained with me, as did what happened in the solarium that night.

The solarium was hexagonal. Entry was provided by three hallways. One hallway came from the outside, and the other two came from the laboratory and the main office wings of the huge building. There was a broad walkway on the main floor of the building that circled the solarium. It connected the offices around its perimeter as well as provided access to an open area on one side where people could relax and talk. Carpeted stairs travelled down from the walkway about 10 feet, ending at a circular floor. Above, the solarium was about 40 feet high, ending in a domed glass roof.

Lying on the stairs, I could see a clear night. The stars were bright enough to shine on the sides of the hexagonal walls, creating patterns of brightness and shadow. At peace in the silent darkness while looking at the beauty of the starlight and smoking a cigarette, my thoughts moved slowly from topic to topic.

I had just begun wondering if our appreciation of things diminished as we learned more about them when there was a glow from someone taking a drag on a cigarette across from me in the darkness.

Reluctant to make noise, I sent across a quiet "Hello."

After a brief pause, a quiet "Hello" came back.

Apparently, Graham, my doctoral advisor was working late, too. Somehow, lying there in the darkness, the constraint which had been between us since I had arrived at the university seemed to go away. I asked him if he believed we lost our sense of wonder when we studied something. He remained quiet for a while, then told me this story.

He and an astronomer friend had been driving across the prairies during the winter. Seeing the Aurora Borealis going crazy, they stopped to watch it for a while, and smoke a cigarette. Graham's friend began talking about how his children would be fascinated by the light display. Graham acknowledged that fact, but he then asked his friend whether his fascination and wonderment had diminished as he studied over the years

After some time passed, his friend said, "How do you think I feel while actually beginning to know what is out there?"

Sitting there in silence, the story made me feel that one's studies should increase interest and wonderment rather than diminish them. Quietly promising myself to approach activities that interested me, rather than those which were thrust upon me, I was beginning to realize how often one could feel things were required of them when they weren't.

After thinking about his friend's reply, I asked Graham if he thought academic study, and the increases in the knowledge that went along with it, reduced the emotionality of the people involved. There were portrayals of scholars being this way, and opinions about the emotional wasteland that could result from academics raising children. (My wife and I had just started raising our young son.) I had seen researchers handling errors and problems that would have driven me up a post. They had done so without emotional outbursts to the point that I came to wonder if they had any feelings at all. The question was not without personal significance. My feelings about where I was and what I was doing were hurting me, and I was wondering what to do about them.

The silence following my question felt loaded. It could be seen as implying criticism of academics, rather than as a question I was hoping for an answer to.

Just as the worry in me was building to acute levels, my mentor said, "You know, the inquisition only had to walk Galileo through an inquisition chamber, then leave him alone for a few days to break him. The average brutalized and uneducated peasant could be walked through without it having much effect at all!"

He went on to tell me that the human brain is the most intelligent one that has evolved, and the most emotional.

Revising my point of view, while lying there in contemplative silence, evolution became a process in which more emotion, rather than less, emerged. Apparently, mother nature had selected for it. I resolved to make an effort to connect with intelligent people in a more positive way, rather than viewing them as unfeeling enemies. It wouldn't prove to be an easy resolution to fulfill, because there can be much intellectual aggression in academe. But eventually, the sense of humour and consideration for others that often accompanies true intelligence won the day with me. In complete contrast to the mass media of the time, I became a little more afraid of unintelligent psychopaths as opposed to intelligent ones. And I learned that successful poker players give smart people things to think and worry about while they are taking their money.

At some time that night, the lessons ended, and we went home. There were no bands playing or momentous cheers. It was just another exhausting day in a lab. All we were doing was resting while having a cigarette in a solarium, and meeting across a gap of estrangement. Who would have thought that such a day and night could have a large effect? My ideas about the nature of learning, intelligence, emotion, evolution, and regression changed following just two short stories and one observation.

The stories Graham told allowed me to see, however briefly, his sensitivity as a human being, as well as the gentler side of his intelligence. As a result, we were destined to reach some positive form of closure, which did happen before his end. What a wonderful thing it is to feel comfortable with someone that you have felt estranged from, and what a sense of loss it could cause. But that wasn't the only thing that was affected by the events that occurred that night.

Many years after leaving the place where I was studying, I began using the phrase "life-changing event in recognition that something small, every day, or apparently unimportant could connect to many things and have a large effect. The saying was reminiscent of the image others have mentioned concerning the change in the whole surface of a pond resulting from waves travelling across its surface after a pebble is dropped into it. Apart from confusing others on occasion because of its obscurity, my saying "life-changing" kept me aware of the possibility of even small things having important effects. Not only that, their effect could also go far enough to create changes in events distant from each other. That is what happened after those night lessons. The ripples spread outside the lab and the solarium.

A few days after that night in the solarium, my wife told me she was concerned about what was happening with our young son. He had butt-propelled before he began walking, and we were amused by it. Others had told us that kids could do that. But, after reaching a stage where he could launch himself from one handhold to another, our boy went back to butt-propelling and was now crawling. Thinking of organismic psychologists who saw regressions as characteristic of normal development, and reflecting on that night in the lab, I reassured my wife that what he was doing was normal. Feeling reassured myself, I went on to say that he would be back to walking in a day or so. And that is exactly what happened. But that wasn't all that arose from the experiences in the lab and solarium. My experiences in the solarium helped change my ideas concerning beauty, and even how I felt concerning a social issue years later while traveling with my son.

Hoping to see a harvest moon, we drove past a long lake one evening where one might see one.

As it turned out, we were lucky, and had been looking at one for about five minutes when my son, said, "Look, dad, the moon is coming for a ride with us!"

I had an immediate impulse to correct him because I was seeing the moon remaining in the same position, with the country around us passing by. Then I realized that he was talking about his own experience. In his world, the moon could ride along with us. As for myself, I had to think a bit to see it that way. The thought added a dimension to the idea that *beauty is in the eye of the beholder.*

While sneaking looks at my son, I recalled the discussion between Graham and the astronomer about his children's fascination with the Aurora Borealis.

I still saw beauty in the child, but now I realized, providing one wanted to think that way, that the astronomer's statements suggested the eye of an adult might see even more beauty than the eye of a child. The adult can see the beauty of the child watching the moon ride along while understanding what is actually happening. What the astronomer had said concerning the Aurora Borealis indicated that the beauty he saw was increased. Surely, we should also extoll the beauty of the adult as well as the child.

Ever since that day, I was convinced that the astronomer's beauty could be larger than that of his children. Of course, I would only say so if forced to. After all, everyone knows kids are beautiful! Personally, the beauty of children and infants is enhanced for me when I see them with their mother or another loving caregiver. It is because of seeing and understanding the love being felt by the adult. Having experienced these simple things and knowing the truth they led to, I wondered about people who would criticize a mother for nursing her child on a bus. What have they failed to learn? Why would they make a social issue out of it? Can't they see the beauty there? Is there something wrong with themselves or wrong within their culture? There may well be.

Years after my son and I were moon watching, I was approached by a nursing student after a lecture I had given. She told me that she was having difficulty with a family she had been assigned to help. The assignment was part of coursework in the nursing program.

She ended by saying: "I think they are regressed."

It was hard to know how to react to such a bold statement. She appeared to be seeing regression as 'the' problem, rather than as part of the family learning to deal with the medical situation they were facing. No doubt the baldness of her statement came from a desire to produce results quickly. Her attitude felt dangerous, to me, because of her apparent need to provide a label and portray regression as the problem. That night in the solarium had reared its head again.

The nursing faculty was hard-working and ran a tight ship. Their standards were high. Their students came to lectures as a group and left as a group. Even their marks were a group being uniformly B and A. Though I hadn't told them, the nursing faculty also occupied a warm spot in my heart by holding the record—personally created by me—for scheduling the most meetings of any faculty in the institution. Despite feeling a bit non-plussed, I simply had to find a way of helping.

Recalling my experiences concerning motor seizure regression and watching my son develop, I quickly scanned the many years and experiences that had since passed and found that my view of regression as part of normal development had remained essentially unchanged. So, I asked the nurse if it would be useful to try and understand how the regression was helping the family deal with the serious medical problem they were facing?

The student was far more open than she sounded during the initial part of our conversation, and she also proved to be a very good observer. Reviewing the family's behaviour, she didn't mention regression once. She even described what she was going to do in order to help them be effective in dealing with the problems they were facing. By this time, I was learning a few things myself, and was beginning to wonder if I really had seen a pathologizing process in her pressure to diagnose and use a label? Later on, I began wondering if medicalizing social problems could be a barrier to solving them, and even put too much social pressure on physicians. These were not easy questions to answer, though I did keep thinking about them. I came to feel that more use might be made of other professions and services outside medicine. The conversation with that intelligent young nurse had opened up a whole new pathway to explore. How I wish I could have watched her next meeting with that family. God bless the nursing faculty; maybe all those meetings were necessary after all.

From time to time, I think of that conversation with the nursing student, and I travel back to that warm, quiet night in the solarium after working late in the lab. I feel so many things while watching the Aurora Borealis with two thoughtful men. The revery progresses to watching my son learn to walk or follow a harvest moon while we are travelling along a highway. Then, my thoughts drift to wondering what questions will confront me next, and what changes I will have to make in order to adapt to them? The changing will never stop. The only thing that will stop it is a final silent darkness.

OFFENDER LEARNING CURVE

Moving On

So, here I was again, sitting at the kitchen table writing another scathing note that would likely remain unsent like all the others. How futile it felt. We were being assessed for teaching performance with $600/year riding on the results. But the procedures being used by the administration were inadequate to support the discriminations they were trying to make. So, at best, the whole enterprise felt like a colossal waste of time and resources. The results of the assessment hadn't hurt me. I was rated as excellent, as opposed to superior, and didn't want to be superior to anybody. Besides, like any teacher trying hard to do his or her job, I had done my own assessments for years. So, I knew "how far I pissed" as one man told me when reacting to my compliment concerning a job he had done. But the state I was in wouldn't prove to be simple any more than the situation would prove to be simple, and the final result of it all would be unexpected.

I was tired of political concerns outweighing methodological rigour in delivering decent education to students. Much of the cost of education was now being paid by students through student loans. While working on the loans committee, it was surprising how virulent people could get in arguing that we were doing students a favour by allowing more loans. I wasn't against helping those in need, but how did we become a country that passed such debts onto its young? Thirteen faculty members in our little institution had gone down the road due to a government initiative, too.

What is one supposed to think of a government that disapproves so strongly of education? The complaining went on and on; yada, yada, yada, and there was no solution in sight.

"Oh, Fred, get off the pot," one might be moved to say. "How long did you go on with the above line?"

Right to the point where my partner said, "You don't have to stay there you know."

The dirge music came to a complete halt as I sat back in my chair. My partner, a successful professional in her own right, had just sent a message. I wasn't alone and everything didn't rest solely on my shoulders. What had been happening over the past years?

I had experienced some good successes for a kid emerging from the east end of Vancouver. Admittedly, my publication record was a bit odd. There was one in a computer user's journal concerning electronic messaging systems in teaching and another doing surgical procedures for an Agriculture Canada study. The study concerned the metabolism of food in different digestive systems. Now, my doctoral dissertation about motor seizure propagation was published in a prestigious journal. And there were several other articles I had written for other journals to go along with that one. There had even been a wonderful sabbatical year in which I had managed to present a poster session at a neurosciences conference in Hollywood. Some neurosurgeons from universities with intimidating names had even kept me overtime with questions. That same conference had been personally important, too. It allowed my old thesis advisor and me to spend time together and finally meet minds and hearts.

My sabbatical ended with a visit from an emeritus professor who took a day to show me the pioneering tests he had created at the university where I was staying during my leave. What a gesture that was!

I'll never forget his advice in response to my questioning attitude as we journeyed together through all his tests:

"You have nothing left to prove, Fred."

It was news to me and still is. This just goes to show—using an often-described idea—one can take the man out of where he came from, but not where he came from out of the man. Nevertheless, it was a well-meant comment, offered by a man who was not only learned, but gracious. Then, there was the fact that my teaching had gotten better over the years. You would think that the dominant feeling with such a record would be one of success instead of botheration. Another thought that might have occurred, but hadn't, was that something was ending.

It took that feeling of botheration after coming home from a sabbatical to start my mind and heart moving away from what I was doing. There was a feeling that I wouldn't be able to top what I had done by staying where I was. It was accompanied by another feeling that I didn't fit in. Looking for a university job or waiting for the college where I was teaching to become a university wouldn't work for me. It would seem that my doctoral advisor was right, that I was an explorer rather than an academician, and I wasn't destined to stay where I was. The time for a change had arrived. How I wished in some ways that it wasn't true! In the end, my feelings were mixed, including, as they did, fear, relief, excitement, gratitude, and finally, acceptance. I gave a year's notice before leaving. In some ways, that last year was the best teaching year I had ever experienced. We even laughed in classes while doing good work.

A Timely Offer

It is possible to have too much experience in one thing when you are pushing 50 years old and looking for a job. I knew that a responsible person would have had one to go to before leaving, but I hadn't seen anything that appealed to me during that last busy year of teaching.

Now, I was appreciating something my brother once told me, "There is a cost to being a Lobo."

I didn't feel like a wolf, but there I was. It was nearing the end of August. The new teaching term was approaching. Classes would start soon, and I had none to teach. Until now, jobs had usually popped up for me. All I had to do was semi-consciously follow the path of least resistance and personal interest, then work hard. No doubt, the approach had allowed me to survive because I had been born into good times. Now, I was older, and I couldn't go back to what I had been doing in previous jobs. I did have a vague plan of working with torture victims, derived partly from reading reports in order to write letters of conscience. As it turned out, however, there were only two specialized programs focusing on helping such victims. The programs were far enough away that the idea of moving to either was very intimidating. One of them was even in a foreign country across the Atlantic, and we were living on Canada's Pacific coast. The little exploratory streak I was carrying didn't stretch that far. There was my partner's professional career to consider, too. I hadn't necessarily expected an easy transition, but vague feelings of anxiety were beginning to form in my viscera.

It was around the beginning of viscera involvement when a friend called me. Knowing I was out of work, he asked if I wanted to do something new.

"Hello, Fred," he said. "Would you like to help create and run a sex offender treatment program?"

"How many people did you phone before me, Dave?" I queried.

"About 20," he replied.

"OK, I'll give it a look," said I.

We laughed. Friends often know more about what is happening with me than I do.

The meeting with Dave and the two other supporters of the proposed enterprise was interesting and filled with enthusiasm. My potential partners were honest, hardworking, and likable people. They inspired confidence. Two of them were also clinicians who could provide supervision for me while I trained. That fact went a long way to allaying one concern I had about what was being proposed. They even offered me as much latitude as possible during the developmental phase and had already found an office in a counselling center that I could use. The office had no windows, but I only had to pay minimal rent. There would even be other counsellors around me to chat and drink coffee with. It was so nice to be needed by this time, that I was having trouble keeping my balance.

The man who had found the grant to create the program, and who would later turn out to be another friend, called it "seed money", which it was. He did, however, promise to stay in the background to provide whatever administrative support was required. The proposal looked like exactly what I needed.

Despite the rush, I'll be damned if the plan didn't work. None of us were seeking personal fame for what we did. My two clinician friends moved on when things were running well, and my administrator friend stayed around to hunt with me for yearly meat. He even found me a contract for a private practice that lasted for years. Our program was eventually taken over by a government agency. They kept me on as a sessional psychologist, helping me re-certify while broadening my skills still further. So, the experience was a personal success, and, in this respect, the world continued to treat me as someone it was looking out for. But I'm still not sure how thankful I am for getting involved in what we created. The devil was in what happened along the way. The learning curve for me was very steep, and the personal changes it caused were far-reaching.

Awakening

On the first day in my new office, I looked up and saw one of the center's counsellors approaching. My steep learning curve was about to begin. Stopping some distance away from me with a tentative air, she said that there was a lay counsellor on the telephone who wanted to refer one of his clients to our program. The mild feeling of challenge I was experiencing rapidly dispersed to be replaced by one of incredulity leavened with a tinge of fear. The counsellor's tentativeness came from knowing, as I did, that we didn't have a program, and I wasn't ready to accept clients. Realizing my hand was now on the non-existent program's steering wheel, however, I didn't run. Accompanying the message bearer out of my office, while wearing my most confident demeanour, I picked up the telephone.

The object of the referral turned out to be a grandfather who had sexually abused his daughters and was now driving his grandkids back and forth to school. It's difficult to adequately describe what listening to that first telephone call felt like. My reaction didn't just come from the nature of the call. It was also driven by the fact that I retrieved one powerhouse of memory in the middle of it. When the memory burst into view, I was thinking that I had never heard of such a thing as a grandfather sexually abusing his daughters, let alone his granddaughters. After its sudden appearance, however, the memory remained present throughout the remainder of the telephone call and the events that followed. How could I have forgotten what had happened?

Have you ever had an experience in which your attention becomes riveted to something, and everything around you begins to cycle through periods of disappearing and reappearing? The counsellor's voice kept coming out of the background. It is a wonder I managed to get through his call as well as I did. You might be able to duplicate the feeling if you are underwater banging two rocks together while trying to listen to music being played on the beach. Luckily, the counsellor was reasonable, and we seemed to agree on a workable plan despite how shaken I was. He accepted my adding Grandfather to our files— we now had a single file in our non-existent program. He also agreed to watch over the grandfather until I returned from the U.S. where I was going for training.

I was still thinking about the referral and the memory that emerged during the telephone call when I saw Marilyn, the supportive manager of the counselling center, and one of the nicer people in the world, approaching my office. After our usual greeting, she asked me what *our* —I told you she was nice — problem was with one of the physicians in the community. When I wondered out loud who the physician could be, she said it was the one treating my prospective client. Apparently, the doctor was very irate and had given the counselling center's staff a hard time. He told her he didn't approve of such "… abusive programs…" and had referred his client to a psychiatrist for treatment. It would take time, training, and experience to understand what I was learning from the experience I was having. After a brief pause to process the *abusive programs* slur, my anger changed to mild relief that the situation had been taken off my hands. Feeling that grandfather was no longer my problem, but was now the physician's, the psychiatrist's, and the counsellor's, I went off naively on my trip to the United States. All I had left to deal with was the events I recalled during the telephone referral from the lay counsellor.

The Memory

Stopping at the kitchen door one day, I heard my mom say to my dad, "Somebody should do something."

Neither of them had turned to look at me. They were staring out of our kitchen window at a neighbour's house across the street. The man in that house was having sex with his young daughter, and somehow the adults in our neighbourhood knew about it. The girl was part of our group. We all used to play games together in a field across the interurban tracks. She had told one of her older brothers what was happening to her, and he told the rest of us. The older boys were excited by what was happening. One of them was even trying to talk her into letting him do it with her, too.

Being a year or two behind the other kids, and just entering my own hormonal rush, I felt confused. What was going on was exciting, but at the same time I felt there was something wrong. As memories continued to surface, I recalled the helplessness Mom and Dad appeared to feel while facing the problem. They believed they should act against what was happening, but they didn't know what to do. Their apparent helplessness bothered me and added to my own confusion. It's a big deal when your parents don't know what to do about something, even when you are in your early teens.

Our playmate soon moved or was moved, away from our neighbourhood. The rest of us continued playing together over at the field, though as time went by and some of them began heating the spoon to joy-pop heroin, our group began to break up. Before that happened, however, her brothers had confirmed what had been going on with their sister and told us that her parents had arranged for her to marry someone kind. As for me, I liked her and remember hoping, in some fragmented way, that she would be okay. Is the memory of a collective sigh of relief in the adults true? Was the 'kindliness' attributed to the person she had been hooked up to a fantasy concocted to assuage our own feelings of guilt and helplessness? Never mind the insight into the sexual status of women the experience provided me later in life.

Memories of our playmate kept coming up after I retrieved that first memory of what I heard while standing in the kitchen door at home. Eventually, I even recalled my playmate's name. The girl had seemed confused by what she was going through back then. She was refusing the older boy who wanted to have sex with her. But she also appeared to be disturbed, or pressured, by her refusal. The memory of what she told me when I asked her what was going on, however, is the most powerful one. I was shy to ask, and she was reluctant to tell me, but she did anyway.

We had met while we were both walking on the pathway beside the small stream that ran through an orchard and a bush near the field we all played in. She was standing facing me with her back to the little stream and a whisp of her blond hair sticking out from the side of her head. She was taller than me, and I was looking up at her. The sun coming through the trees was shining through that wisp of hair and outlining her head and body as she told me how she kept hitting her stomach to prevent herself from becoming pregnant while her father was 'doing it'. My feelings at the time must have been strong, but what she said seems cloaked in a kind of roaring sound. I believe she did hit her tummy while he was raping her, and I will always believe it.

Training

Learning is not a neutral act and when a person learns something many factors come into play. One's thinking and how one feels change. (I forget the teacher's name who told me this, but he said that when one learns to use a hammer his or her way of thinking about a hammer changes and so does the way they feel about it. The thought stuck and has remained with me ever since.) So, how does one prepare to enter training to work with sexual offending in the middle 1980s? I accepted that I was in for something new that would change me and took it as an article of faith that I would survive. After all, I had learned quite a bit by this time and managed to survive as well as acquire a good grounding in basic psychological processes. There were also people supporting me in the community at the clinical and administrative levels. Looking back, the situation would be laughable if it wasn't so serious. The changes would be personal and far more powerful than anything I could anticipate.

It was a time when only isolated counsellors were dealing with sex offenders in our province. The social milieu surrounding such offences was rapidly changing and feminist political activism was very prevalent. With predictable and somewhat boring enthusiasm, the topic was picked up by mass media with the usual distortions for emotional effect with terms like pedophile becoming more salient. To me, there seemed to be an increase in the use of pejorative terms concerning the male roles in society too. At the same time, knowledge concerning sexual offending itself was increasing. We were finding out that the number of assaults was higher than previously reported and that offenders could have more than one form of offending in their history as well as cross over in the kind of victimization they were attracted to. Incest offending could involve children outside the home and the number of assaults on a victim in such cases could be high. There were instances where a rapist might begin as a voyeur, and a diagnosed homo pedophile had also assaulted a female child. These might be regarded as dated observations and someone who is interested in pursuing such knowledge should consult current research journals and people who are presently working in the field. This narrative concerns what happened as I pursued knowledge in the 80s and 90s and the personal impact it had on me.

Most of the early cases I was presented with involved child molestation and that bias will continue here. Restricting ourselves to child molestation is not as limiting as it might sound. Various kinds of sexual offending, including child molestation, followed a repetitive pattern that could be described using a sequence originally derived by individuals working in the area of substance abuse. The offending cycle I learned to use was written in this way:

$$AB \longrightarrow R+ \; Tr \longrightarrow R- \; Push \longrightarrow R+$$

'A' refers to situations and conditions that preceded the offending; 'B' is the individual's offending behaviour; 'R+' refers to rewards the offender receives from the offence, 'Tr' is thoughts of reality or realistic thinking that emerges after the offence; 'R-' is the negative feelings coming from the offender having such realistic thoughts; 'Push' refers to how the offender gets rid of his or her realistic thoughts and 'R+' is the reward he or she receives from getting rid of the negative feelings from having such thoughts. The sequence then repeats at some time in the future. Entries made under each heading could be extensive, and the categories under each could differ depending upon a number of factors, but the purpose of using this pattern during assessment and treatment was always the same. It provided the therapist and the offender a way of understanding how the offending occurs as well as a basis for preventing re-offence. The equation represents part of the thinking I will describe later concerning the grandfather referred to our program.

Many trips for development and training over the years were helpful and challenging. But the first trips to the west coast of the U.S. and the Midwest had elements of the worst and the best experiences. Learning about the area I was to work in during those early travels represented a total emersion in the sexual offending world. It compressed many intense and difficult experiences into a few months and most concerns outside working in the area diminished or seemed to disappear. I had to work hard not only to process what I was learning intellectually but to deal with its emotional impact. The first training program I attended was seven days long with activities during the days and evenings. It provides the best illustration of what the experience was like.

The program seemed straightforward enough. During the day I studied intake, interviewing, and individual counselling, and learned about specialized testing in the field. There was at least one personal counselling session with a therapist to help me deal with issues that could arise while working in the sexual offending area. At night, I attended offender treatment groups as well as a group for wives and significant others. (Later, I would continue to attend such groups including those for victims of sexual assault when the opportunities arose. Attending them helped me keep my head straight concerning offending and its effects. It also allowed me to give something back by describing offender treatment.) When I wasn't involved in group activities during the evenings, I spent hours reviewing tapes of Modified Aversive Behavioural Rehearsal (MABR) sessions. There was little time for socializing with those people who were providing instruction. Looking back, I feel a sense of personal isolation during those early months despite having the periodic company of my life partner and those who were helping me develop the program in my hometown.

Training during that first trip began with attending an evening sex offender treatment group on the day I arrived. While heading to the group, I saw a slightly built, middle-aged woman wearing a floral print dress sitting on a chair in the hallway. She had her hands on top of the purse in her lap and appeared quiet, removed, and demure to me—for some reason, the impression and that word 'demure' have stuck with me over all these years. Her husband was finishing an interview with one of the institution's counsellors in the office across from where she was sitting. I didn't know it when I saw her, but he would be petitioning for entry to the treatment group, which I would soon be observing. She was probably confronting her own denial concerning her husband's sexual offending while sitting on that bench. The courts had found him to be guilty, and in the system in which I was beginning to learn, he had chosen treatment under community supervision rather than jail time. (I was later told that some did choose jail.) The lady in the hall, her husband being interviewed and I, were all approaching our own instructional activities. The feelings are faint, but I believe I can still imagine her shock, confusion, grief, and rage.

One purpose of the group that evening would be to consider the husband's petition for membership. He would attend the group that evening, and its members had a final say in whether he would be allowed to join the group for treatment. They went through all of their usual activities with the candidate present before considering his application. The session began with the election of a member to run the meeting and he facilitated what went on during the session from that point on. All members of the group were elected to do this at one time or another. The institutional therapist remained in the background throughout the process. I was surprised by how quickly and efficiently the election of the leader went.

Two men briefly described what the group would cover during the meeting if they ran it. After a quick show of hands, one was elected, and he ran the meeting from that point on. Each member of the group did a layout of his offences and presented any issues that had emerged during the previous week. The meeting then followed along the lines the elected leader had suggested. There wasn't any handwringing as the meeting went on. What was happening was very real and as serious as cancer. It struck me at the time, that the way things were being done supported taking the problem of sexual offending seriously as well as providing concrete, as opposed to abstract, personal support in resolving problems. Such an approach helped break down denial and encouraged workable solutions to problems as well as personal ownership of one's offending.

The final task for that evening was dealing with the petition for membership. There wasn't any handwringing during that event either. The elected leader continued to run the group and the members of the group applied what they knew about sexual offending while interviewing the petitioner. He may have been able to fool others around him in the community enough to remain safe for years, but he was not able to fool the group members. The therapist monitoring the group still remained largely in the background. He did have the benefit of interviewing the candidate prior to the group and might intervene if the members went off-track.

One such intervention by the monitoring therapist went something like this: "We're going off track, and this man is here paying hard-earned money to deal with his problem."

I recall seeing a reaction by the men in the group to the statement. It was true that they were paying to be there, and they did have the right to expect good treatment. Paying appeared to make a difference to them. You don't seem to find many rich people in sex offender groups and even a small amount could be significant for most of them. After all these years, I still believe that clients paying for a small part of treatment costs makes a difference in therapy.

The candidate for entry to the group, who undoubtedly had experienced an earful of input while watching the earlier activities, responded to the milieu surrounding him. I did too, and what happened was a revelation for me. The questioning was assertive and dealt directly and concretely with the applicant's offences. (Abuse or vilification of the person would be viewed as something that perpetuates an offending cycle and it would not be tolerated.) Much of the questioning was directed toward achieving a good description of the candidate's sexual offending as well as his attitude toward it. I found myself forming an impression of both.

The petitioner identified more victims and increased the number of assaults committed against the single victim he was charged with. In fact, the number of offences he had committed was seriously under-estimated compared to what he was convicted of. So ended the one victim-one offence theory. As the meeting went on, I kept thinking to myself; surely not more, but more victims continued to emerge, and the frequency of offences increased as the questioning by the group members continued. Not only that I could find no reason to doubt the truth of what was being found. Personal ownership of one's offending was required. There was no room for excitement or storytelling for the purpose of status enhancement. The man applying for entry that evening was accepted into the group on a provisional basis.

As for me, sexual offending was becoming real in my thinking, and I was realizing that it recurred far more often than I thought it did. It was surprising how active offenders had been once better facts became available. My feelings of shock and incredulity intensified while studying MABR tapes.

Modified Aversive Behavioural Rehearsal

During MABR sessions the offender was filmed while he portrayed what he did during offending and explained his actions as he went along. A therapist asked the client questions to facilitate the process. The purpose of the exercise was to facilitate acceptance of his responsibility for his offending and to help him describe his offending pattern. An individual knowing the pattern of his or her offending was viewed as central to preventing it from reoccurring. The films were instructive but very hard to watch. They provided a stark picture.

In one film, for example, the offender portrayed how he molested his daughter while she was on the telephone talking to her friends. The thing that sticks most in my mind from that session was when he said to his daughter, "You know that all you have to do to get me to stop is to hang up the phone."

He was illustrating how he not only set her up to be offended but how he kept her responsible for what was going on. I can't describe how I felt while watching this. The thought kept hammering through my head that I had never realized just how important friends were to a young child until that moment. It was a deflective, defensive thought.

Participating in sex offender groups and viewing MABR tapes showed me how deficient my awareness had been concerning sexual offending. I haven't believed in limiting myself to data collected solely based on individual interviews, court, or jail records since that time. And I certainly don't rely on mass media reports. I was starting to live in a very different world than the one I was used to. What I was seeing not only repulsed me, but it also created a powerful rage. At first, my rage was internal and directed at the offenders. But I was becoming aware that such rage should be directed toward the offending and the factors that cause it to happen, not the offender. A thought formed that *to act in any other way makes us responsible for perpetuating the very thing we want to stop.*

Returning

I don't remember much about my return trip from the U.S., which may be the best measure of how overwhelmed I was. In the past, I had found that changes in thought and feeling were to be expected when entering new situations. But this time the impact was most powerful, and the shocks continued. I felt out of step with activities and with the people around me. It took time for me to become comfortable interacting with those who weren't offenders, weren't working with offenders, or couldn't empathize with the state such work had put me in.

My mind now contained templates describing the pattern of such offences and their reality was undeniable. On one hand, there was no doubt that the knowledge was helpful. It helped me to know what to look for, what to listen to, and how to approach what was there when dealing with the problem. But that kind of knowledge changes one's own internal and external life markedly—at least it did mine.

It was shocking how my reaction to people using personal defences in everyday life changed. I readily accepted the idea that defences such as denial and rationalization were part of a sex offender's offence cycle. But I missed the potential impact of this knowledge upon myself. And I didn't anticipate my reaction when others used such defences in everyday life.

I came to see all of us as being similar to sex offenders in our use of such defences when, up until then, I had offenders nicely housed in a separate group. I didn't like this fact one damned bit, and the comparison could come up in any number of situations.

I told myself something like this: "Bullshit! Do you know where such thinking can lead?"

The experience happened more often than one might expect. People often deny evidence or rationalize holding a view in the face of negative evidence. Sometimes they are even right to do so. But at other times their defences can lead to a failure to resolve a situation or even result in re-introducing the same conditions they are protesting. The view sounds extreme, I know, but think of extreme measures in other cases. How about burning people at the stake to bring them to God's love? Or using racist thoughts and actions to eliminate racism. I knew that my internal impulses to speak out in such ways would be inappropriate. So, usually, I didn't speak. But I felt under pressure from such feelings and thoughts for quite some time.

Another situation I found difficult to deal with was my own rage. It is simply true that sexual offenders are quite helpless in the face of society's wrath. Adopting an approach of beating them, vilifying them, or using hatred of them for personal gain, whether psychological, political, or economic is helping perpetuate a cycle of abuse. There were external forces at work here. The media, for example, became part of the situation. It wasn't necessarily forward in advocating killing, raping and torturing child molesters. But the indirect advocating of such an approach was often done by using threats of such. When I watched someone in a popular TV series, for example, breaking the law for revenge, or threatening an offender with what is going to happen to him–rape– in jail in order to extract information, for example, I often thought of this. It is an interesting approach, isn't it? It keeps those using the approach innocent of actually committing, or directly advocating such horrible acts. But it allows them (or us?) to enjoy the acts vicariously by locating their occurrence in jails where they are done by people who we don't approve of. What convenient targets sex offenders are, and how easy it is to justify hating them and abusing them. And how satisfying it can feel to have others apply actions toward them that we wouldn't engage in during our everyday lives if only in movies, newspapers and on TV.

The above does not mean sexual offenders are not dangerous. They certainly are. Child molesters, for example, who historically were viewed as weaklings and not particularly dangerous are certainly dangerous toward children. Nor is what I am saying intended to mean that we shouldn't act against such behaviour. At its simplest, such offending is a big guy picking on a little guy to satisfy his or her own needs and wants. We learned how wrong this could be in the sandboxes when we were kids. But I came to feel that one must be very careful how they went about opposing such offending. One should continually strive to apply a social policy, as opposed to satisfying a need for personal revenge.

One of the first signs I ran into that I was in error was separating sexual offenders from the rest of us. If such splitting off becomes necessary with a problem, it should be done with gravitas and mourning, not accompanied by feelings of violence, self-righteousness, and rage. In other words, we should deal with our own problems first before trying to deal with other people's. But where does one put one's rage and the desire for a 45-cent—the cost of a bullet—solution? I worked hard at eventually sublimating mine into supporting treatment and being concerned for the safety of victims. Revenge movies and TV programs were put in the round file where they belong. It's a difficult job because one doesn't want to become an automaton and lose personal disapproval of bad behaviours and poor social policy either. Am I arguing in favour of the existence of a certain moral tension while doing the job? I believe that I am.

It may not surprise you that such ideas as trust, forgiveness, and promises took on a different hue for me after experiencing that first training period. Trust became a five-letter word, and the first thing a con artist asks for. Promises, without the knowledge to effectively back up the promise being made, became empty. Forgiveness became an 11-letter word, but it was a bit of a special case. For one thing, there was the idea that a victim should forgive an offender to become healthy. Did it somehow derive from Christ's or God's ability to forgive?

"Fine," I said to myself. "Leave the forgiving to the two who can legitimately do it."

The purpose of forgiveness isn't to be a get-out-of-jail-free card. It is to give the person the strength to tackle the problem they are facing.

Don't require victims to forgive offenders. It puts the onus for action in the wrong place, by making the victim do something. It also provides an avenue for the offender to transfer blame to the victim for not forgiving him. Why would one put such stress on a victim, especially when their main task is to overcome the effect of what has been done to them? If they aren't successful at doing that, they can fail to fulfill their potential as humans and even turn into offenders themselves. Do you find this to be too simple? Simplicity isn't always wrong. Concreteness is one thing that offenders who are successful in avoiding reoffence apply to sexual offending. Abstraction can be dangerous. Watch out for nice, comfortable discussions about victims not being able to get better if they don't forgive someone. Ask yourself who is being treated if you feel good about the idea.

So, trust, promises, and forgiveness had to be replaced by other approaches, but that didn't change the fact that my external world changed. I came to associate sexual offences with virtually any town or city in our province and a lot of other places too. What a difference! Such crimes existed not only across social and cultural strata but were distributed throughout our home province and even worldwide. The name of a place would be mentioned and up would pop a memory of an offence. The fishing, food and scenic wonders were still there, but now the sexual offending was, too. My impression of those places became less pleasant. In fact, some of those memories still present themselves from time to time, even though much of the heat in them has gone away. I can even recall the name of the town that I designated as our provincial incest capital in British Columbia, and the country in the world I thought most of the pedophiles visited when on holiday.

The Secret I Must Have Known I Had

You might think that after all of the soul-searching and scrutiny of beliefs, things would be pretty much over. They weren't. In fact, a group of us were in a seminar studying the role of female therapists in sex offender treatment, when I disclosed my secret and embarrassed myself at the same time.

In a fit of possibly inappropriate sharing, I blurted out: "Hey you know what? I retrieved a memory of being sexually molested by the school nurse in Grade Eight. It must have been a sexual offence."

For some reason, my mind had started going back to Grade Eight in high school. I was in Spanish class when a very unpleasant spasm in my nether regions struck me—the physician who eventually saw me said it was my vas deferens that was acting up. That is a region that would be of concern to a male in Grade Eight, probably even one in Grade 100. Too shy to call out, and paralyzed by the pain and fear, I sat there, remaining silent until the class left. The student that would normally sit where I was when the next class came in must have taken another seat. The new teacher took some time to notice I was there. When she did finally see me and found out what was happening, she had two of the boys in the class carry me to the school nursing station.

A male physician was called in but, in the guise of doing a medical exam, the nurse who made me comfortable on the cot in her room fondled my genitals. I remembered seeing her breathing heavily and how she stroked my penis—yup, it became engorged. In fact, I was unaware of anything that would stop such engorgement at that age. She also gently squeezed my testicles and felt the tubes connecting to them; legitimate actions, right? I did not, however, feel blessed by what she did. Nor did I feel her actions were legitimate. In fact, the thought I had while watching her breathing hard was significant: *She wanted to be a doctor but couldn't hack it.* Nevertheless, I was reluctant to tell anyone what had happened and never had. I just lay there until the physician finally came and repeated the exam without stroking. The nurse silently watched the physician tap my erection with a pen. Yes, it had come back up again, but it went down almost immediately after the tap. How fast I de-tumesced struck me as funny and embarrassing at the same time. Was the nurse's silence due to innocence by association with authority? Or was her behaviour a reflection of knowing how young babies could be stopped from crying? Being male at that age made the idea of being a victim unacceptable to me. My view, while not particularly complicated, was that it was her problem, and her weakness, not mine. But I kept quiet about it for many years, didn't I, and I was embarrassed by the disclosure I made in that seminar. My reluctance to disclose what had happened helped me to empathize with the reluctance of victims to report their abuse.

The assault by the nurse also created a bias in me toward females, though I followed a complicated pathway in finally accepting this. Up until my disclosure in the seminar, I would have denied that I was biased against women. I even had some smug feelings about how hard I had laboured to become so liberal and treat them equally. Naturally, I had a number of cogent arguments to support my view, including the fact that I had so little difficulty in adjusting to feminist consciousness-raising exercises. I just experienced the odd surprise that came from them, like unintentionally assuming a doctor would be male, for example, as helping me develop as a person. So, where was the bias? Eventually, I noticed that it came into play with women in positions of authority. It is natural, of course, to be aware of the potential of powerful people in positions of authority to do harm. But I could more easily accept males in positions of authority than I could females. And I found myself holding women in such positions to higher standards. I even found tinges of stereotyping in how I celebrated female successes.

Many of the feelings I had concerning men and women came under scrutiny while working with sexual offenders. The feminist activism that was happening at the time made it politically useful to attack males as "dead beat dads" and "sex offenders." Such attacks hurt me as a male, and I found myself to be quite vulnerable to them. Much of the vulnerability came from the fact I was busily finding out that male sexual offending was real. Such a reality embarrassed me. It even reduced my happiness with being male.

For me, there was a feeling of unfairness surrounding the issue of singling out males for negative social treatment and blaming. Evidence suggested that females and males abused children at approximately the same rates, with males sexually abusing children more often, and female abusiveness tending more toward physical and psychological abuse. I knew there were female sexual offenders and had acquired a modicum of information about programs for their treatment. They were generally treated as victims, except in some programs to the south of us. There were also biases in other court situations that favoured females. I recall being invited to a meeting of lawyers practicing family law, for example, in which the majority of lawyers present acknowledged how much easier it was to represent women in familial conflicts. There was evidence that women were sentenced more lightly for some crimes than men, too. I was finding the position of gender in our culture to be rife with inconsistencies and errors.

Certainly, the situation with the school nurse had some effect. But was I a misogynist, or am I? I don't think so, and neither does my heart. There are differences between men and women, and we all apply social judgments to them. My feelings of unfairness and vulnerability, however, didn't come from believing there weren't legitimate concerns behind female activism. It was more that I saw our purpose to be more one of elevating the power and status of women than one of reducing the power of men and blaming them for society's problems. I was also suspicious of the presentation of women as powerless victims that seemed to be going on. The view might have been politically useful in the short term, but I wondered what the long-term effect would be. My view was opposed to that held by radical feminists who believed that males should be disempowered. The men I was seeing were the least powerful of males, and their offending came from powerlessness, rather than having personal power.

My bias concerning women in authority didn't go away when I became aware that I had one, though my view of it changed. In fact, it proved to be necessary to apply counter-measures just to arrive at a balanced view when such reared its ugly head. Comparing the social biases being applied to females with those being applied to males helped. In the long term, consciousness-raising didn't just apply to my view of females; it also applied to my view of males. A feeling of personal freedom accompanied the realization, though I suspected there were better ways of going about solving our social problems. And that, I submit, is where personal success with abuse can get a person to. Some of its effects remain, and it takes some personal vigilance to deal with them.

Grandfather Returns

So, what about the grandfather? What was going on with him? It will be necessary to guess some of the answers based on my experiences over the years. Prior to my leaving on that first trip to the U.S., a physician placed an obnoxious and misinformed telephone call to the counselling center after sending Grandfather off to see a psychiatrist. I felt relieved as well as mildly disgruntled by what was said, but readily transferred responsibility for the grandfather's treatment to the physician, psychiatrist, and lay counsellor involved. Ignorance is bliss.

On my first day back, there was a telephone call from the lay counsellor that jarred that comfortable ignorance. The problem surrounding the old referral re-emerged, and I had left important things undone.

The counsellor said, "I called to tell you that Grandfather is still transporting his grandkids. He told me it was OK and that he was in treatment. How is he doing?"

I hadn't told the counsellor about what had occurred with his referral. Nor had I told him about the physician referring Grandfather to a psychiatrist.

After I explained this to him, he asked, "Did you call the psychiatrist to make sure he got there?"

I was back in training again. I hadn't called the psychiatrist. The major concern for the counsellor and me was the safety of the children. And the sex offender would be unlikely to discuss transporting his grandkids with a psychiatrist treating him for depression. We were afraid that they were in need of protection. Their grandfather might already be offending them or grooming[13] them. He had already done so with his daughters, and they hadn't received help. Not only that, the counsellor wasn't satisfied that he and the grandfather had dealt with the grandfather's sexual offending satisfactorily during their sessions together.

My initial impulse was to take over responsibility for any further action because of the referral the counsellor had made, and, let's face it, because of my having screwed up, too. The counsellor readily agreed. He appeared to be hoping that I would take over. And contacting a social worker and/or the psychiatrist, who was supposedly providing treatment, were our two options. The former would be a member of

---

[13] Grooming is a term used to describe how a sex offender sets up his or her victims for abuse. Being alone with them, and separating them from others, is part of the pattern. Such separating is usually done both physically and psychologically.

the group designated to handle cases in which children were in need of protection. An interview by such a trained social worker would establish whether the abuse was occurring. One caveat, however, was that all the information I had was indirect. I didn't know for sure that the grandfather was offending, but only suspected it was likely. I also hadn't interviewed him and any treatment relationship I had with him was distant, to say the least. So, the first step I took was to call the psychiatrist.

He was reluctant to provide information about his client, though he did confirm that Grandfather came to his office.

Not wanting to waste time, I got right to the point. "I understand Grandfather was referred to you by doctor [I used full names for both]. He was originally referred to me concerning a problem with sexual offending against his children. A counsellor [again using the correct name] told me that the grandfather was transporting his grandchildren while saying it is OK to do so because he is getting treatment. I am making sure he was successful in getting to your office, as well as ensuring you are aware of what is being reported about him."

There was silence on the other end of the line. It was beginning to look like the information I had provided had created a large problem.

After a long delay, he said in a strained voice, "I'm not treating Grandfather for sexual offending. I'm treating him for depression."

What can we see from his statement? It is pretty clear that dealing with Grandfather's sexual offending wasn't included in treatment at all. I didn't necessarily disagree with using antidepressants in treating sexual offenders. In fact, there was a view, which made sense to me at the time, that reducing depression, or dealing with a substance abuse problem, could help in a sex offender's treatment. What I didn't approve of was avoiding the issue and leaving an offender in the community who wasn't taking responsibility for his offending and who hadn't learned a strategy to avoid reoffending. There is a difference between being an expert in offending, as Grandfather seemed to be, and being an expert in avoiding offending, as Grandfather couldn't be. I came to think in a similar fashion concerning substance abuse, too. Promises not to abuse substances were hollow without knowledge and understanding of ways to avoid using them.

An offender getting helpers to deal with one problem to avoid dealing with another is an old dodge. Let's imagine what had likely been going on.

Grandfather was probably frightened when his counsellor told him that a sex offender treatment program was being started. So, he took immediate steps to protect himself by going to his physician and telling him how depressed and upset he was. Judging from the physician's subsequent reactions, Grandfather was even shrewd enough to appeal to the doctor's personal and professional biases. The net result of his actions, apart from leaving all the problems of sexual offending for his victims to solve, was to get a referral, avoid dealing with his offences, and receive drug treatment that would help him feel better. Of course, the approach didn't do much to protect the children or help his daughters. The psychiatrist may well have acted differently, but he had received a referral for depression and was unaware of the grandfather's sexual offending.

Until the creation of the sex offender program, things had probably been going the way Grandfather wanted them to. He had committed a crime and had kept himself safe from the legal consequences of his acts. No one was actively treating his daughters for the abuse they endured. Treatment of his victims would provide a source of information about his offending and be very threatening for him. It could result in criminal charges being brought against him, and would also result in a description of the damage his offending had done. That he had done damage would be a thought he would strongly wish to avoid. In the same way, Grandfather's own treatment would be a source of information about his offending and threaten the view he was trying to maintain, that he didn't have a problem. According to the counsellor, his daughters had demanded he get counselling, and the problem of Grandfather's sexual offending remained unresolved. What I suspected is that counselling had not only failed to resolve the issue, but that it had likely provided the grandfather with another means of keeping his daughters helpless—remember that young girl on the telephone?

What about the role of the two abused daughters in all this? Again, I will have to fall back on what I learned over the years, rather than direct evidence. The victims had forced their father to take counselling and that was probably why he went. But the daughters then went on and failed to protect their own children from a potentially hazardous situation. Having been abused makes most things harder to achieve and it doesn't provide you with the training necessary to be a good protector or a good formulator of social policy.

Even more importantly, consider the conditions the two victims appeared to be operating under. Neither of the most powerful professionals involved with Grandfather—the physician and the psychiatrist—had communicated with them. They had not received professional help for the assaults and violation of trust they had endured. These things alone indicated how isolated they were. (One of the truly ugly things to see in such situations can be when the rest of the family rejects the victim and blames them for lying and having problems.) Imagine the lack of information about victimization and offending that isolation of the victims creates, and how alone they must be. Grandfather, of course, was telling them how well he was doing in counselling. Would they consider the possibility he was grooming or offending their children? They might, but imagine the distress a serious contemplation of the idea would bring to them. Clearly, it would be much more palatable to deny their father's dangerousness and emphasize his success in counselling.

A question I asked myself about Grandfather was how aware he was of processes that occurred in his victims, and how he kept them responsible for what happened? One fact that struck me was how his daughters hadn't reported his offending against them. I knew it was very difficult for victims to report being abused. But I was also aware that reporting was more likely to be done by a victim when they were trying to protect someone they cared about. One question that Grandfather would be asked in an effective treatment group was how he avoided being reported when he began abusing his second daughter. I suspect that Grandfather was very good at manipulating people and at turning off his daughter's impulses to tell on him. In the end, I never got a chance to ask him. I left Grandfather to the care of the psychiatrist who was now informed, responsible for the treatment and how it was reported.

Was I correct in leaving things there? Am I writing fiction?

At one time, I wouldn't have believed such a convoluted story. My life began filling with such stories. I would face descriptions of reoffences after private treatment and stories in which treatment was used as a tool to avoid being caught. In one verifiable story, an abused mother with an alcohol problem would leave her young son with her homo-pedophile boyfriend while she was out drinking. I met the son in a jail where he was serving a sentence for assaulting her because she called him a "queer." He was a mess at any level one might wish to think about. Victimized people aren't exempt from going to jail. In fact, many of the sex offenders I saw reported being sexually abused themselves.

Right now, I am recalling my incredulity while watching MABR tapes. In some ways, such stories have never entirely gone away. Sexual offending is a very different arena to work in than one in which someone is looking forward to learning something when they are in college. Or, where someone has a problem and genuinely wants to work on solving it.

Doubt

Offending is repetitive, and offenders learn what works through experience, fantasizing, and repetition. When you run up against someone that has developed repetitive offending in this way, they knowingly, or automatically, apply things that conditioning has taught them work. They can fool you every bit as much as they can fool themselves. That is part of how sexual offenders assault people and remain uncaught. And it's how they can fool treatment personnel and other reasonably intelligent people. I once saw a judge, a crown counsel, and a defence counsel who were stymied by an offender who was mentally challenged. Let's be clear about this. These were decent, hard-working, intelligent, and very experienced men. I doubt they would be halted by any problem for long. They also had the reputation of being very good in the venue they worked in. The offender, in this case, was dogmatically claiming, against all evidence to the contrary, that he didn't do the offending. The difficulty for the three professionals involved with the case was that they could see no reason why the offender persisted in denying his guilt. *Contrary to the opinion of some, those working in the court system are very good at determining the truth in a situation. They also tend to be people who care about what they are doing.* Given the irrefutability of the evidence, the offender's denial simply didn't make sense to them. So, they decided to see if they had missed something.

Being with such a sophisticated company in a small room was pretty challenging, even intimidating. In fact, I was relieved when I realized that the councillors were tangling with a special subgroup of offenders that were at high risk for impulsive offending. Because of their mental challenges, defences in such offenders tended to be comparatively simple. In this case, simple, repeated denial appeared to be what had worked for the person prior to being caught. He was automatically repeating it because creating more sophisticated defences was very difficult, if not impossible, for him. While such offenders can be satisfying to work with, they require repetitive, multi-modal forms of teaching during treatment, as well as requiring knowledgeable, long-term supervision by those close to them. Describing the individual's special needs, and why such people use comparatively simple defences, helped in adjudicating the situation. In a way, the counsellors were fooled by their own sophistication.

What happened in the court situation I have described suggests we should be careful in our views concerning offending and offenders, especially when they are based on other people's opinions, occur outside the courtroom, and are based on material presented in the mass media. As with many situations in life, this helps preserve a balanced perspective.

I found that sexual offending does exist and can happen in people close enough to us to create difficulty in having a clear, or accurate, perspective. I came to believe that, in general, offenders are no smarter or dumber than the rest of us. They are human beings who have done something wrong and are fighting to protect themselves. Not only that, but they have often learned how to keep offending without being caught. I came to rely on the judicial system to determine guilt or innocence and to create the supervision conditions allowing for adequate treatment with supervision to reduce risk to the community. That system was able to do such things better than any other agency I was aware of.

Two Cases

It feels like we have been on a long journey. So, I am going to leave you with two stories suitably modified to protect identities. The first case presented itself while I was thinking about how Keats was right when he said, "Beauty is truth," and how the second part concerning truth being beautiful was true only some of the time.

It was quite late in my career when I was asked to sit with the sex offender I want to describe. The authorities had removed him from jail to die of cancer in more comfortable surroundings. The man had many victims, including his own children. The first time we met, he spent our meeting talking at me about the crimes he had been accused of and how everyone had lied about him. I was frozen in place listening to him. Considering the counselling he had received in jail; his denial was unexpected. To me, he seemed to be wasting what little time he had left. Then, I realized that I was hoping for some kind of mushy ending—an act of redemption in which he would valiantly arise from his bed in the face of his pain and fess up. Accepting responsibility for what he had done, he would help to remove the pain from his victims. He would say to them that he had done wrong, and it wasn't their fault. He would tell them he was learning to avoid repeating what he had done. He might apologize, but knowing forgiveness is something that should only be offered freely, would avoid putting his arm on them for it. I would have gladly carried the message to them myself.

My god, I thought with some considerable shock. *All these years, and I am still a Pollyanna.*

He had been through religious forgiveness and cognitive-behavioural treatment. He was a victim and an offender, and he had decided to stay there. It was all other people's fault. There was no remorse, and nothing left in him but resentment of his own abuse and those that lied about him. He was running out of time. I didn't see what else to do, but to sit there listening while being as kind as I was able.

Our hours the next day were spent in the same way. Even in the throes of death, he was dishonest. On the third visit, I found out from the caretakers that he had died early that morning. To me, his was an ugly, untruthful death. He died irrevocably blocked by his inability to face what he had done, or what was done to him. There was no metaphysical structure that I could see—no personal understanding I could arrive at—that would suggest any redemption.

The second case was quite different. It occurred even closer to the end of my working days and took place in a jail where I had occasionally done assessment and counselling. The referral was different from what I was used to. The guards and administrators sounded like they were personally concerned for the inmate. Of course, it wasn't unusual for guards or administrators in a prison to be professionally concerned about the safety of a sexual offender. Violence between inmates was something they were supposed to prevent, and sex offenders could be targets. Such concerns were also based on economic factors. Convenient targets like sex offenders might require removal from the open range and be contained in more expensive special housing. No one wins if violence occurs on the open range. Nevertheless, I still felt that something was different this time around. As was said to me, the inmate was "... over 80, and a nice old guy..." The main concern of those taking care of him was that he wouldn't be able to protect himself. The 'nice old guy' part caused some internal vibrations in me. What was I letting myself in for?

During the interview, the old fellow and I began by talking about whether he was safe. He assured me he was OK, even going on to tell me he was well-liked by the other inmates as well as the guards. His view seemed to be correct. So, I moved our discussion to why he was in prison. Whereupon he laid out a perfect sexual-offending scenario, describing how he lured little girls into his workshop and managed to "tickle" their vaginas. He even went on to tell how he made them giggle while doing so. The impression I had that he loved the little girls wasn't new to me. It wasn't all that unusual for a child molester to report loving a victim. But, for some reason, the statements from the old man had a different effect on me. I didn't even confront the minimization implicit in the word 'tickle'. Is a narcissistic offender capable of loving someone? Whatever was going on, my reflexive negative answer to the question was being eroded.

The old fellow described how he found new victims, and even went on to tell me how he used previous victims to help things along. Now, by this late stage of my career, I didn't automatically like or dislike offenders. But, God help me, during the interview I was beginning to like this old fellow while feeling a need to resist it. I am sure he could see the struggle I was having in keeping my feelings separate from concentrating on what was happening inside and outside our meeting. When our time was up, I wished him well and thanked him for talking to me. I told him I would report that he was safe in remaining where he was but went on to say to him that I would also write that he needed supervision when he left prison. Moving toward the door, he looked like an old guy who was puzzled and trying to think something through. I believe he even rubbed the back of his neck, though I am not sure whether that perception is my subconscious acting up. Stopping with a hand on the doorknob, he turned to look at me.

I will never forget what he said. "You know, I told all of them that I was not a sex offender. But you know what—I am, aren't I?"

Then, turning back, he went off into the hallway. Anyone who has worked with or is working with sexual offenders will probably think about that last statement. Against all my inclinations, vestiges of my liking for him somehow remain. I'm still thinking about that last sentence, too.

GOOD ADVICE

The building I was heading toward housed people who had already committed a crime or were being tried for such. Typically, there was an insanity concern associated with their containment. Things had been going well during these early days of my practicum. There had been only one rather painful exception to an otherwise rosy picture. The head nurse noticed that I had put a file back into a filing cabinet, rather than leaving it out for her to re-file. Apparently, the sin I had committed was the way files became lost. The way she applied the thumbscrews had left no doubt concerning the enormity of what I had done. I did survive by pleading a desire to help but would never again treat a file the way I had. Since that time a month or so ago, I hadn't committed any of the myriads of other bad things one could do. Perhaps, I was overdue.

There were the usual greetings after reaching the nursing station, followed by the question concerning who I was going to see. I told the team a name, which resulted in a mildly loaded silence.

Being just smart enough to know I should listen to front-line troops, I asked, "OK, you guys, what's going on?"

It was a bit like pulling teeth without an anesthetic, but I finally got the story. They were reluctant to give it because they didn't want to muck around with the director level that had sent me over. To them, I was still a testee, not a tester. They were also a good-hearted bunch, and their silence was my cue to probe further. It turned out that the powers-that-be had assigned a client to me who no one had been able to test—an assessment usually involved interviews, personality tests, and intelligence tests. The nursing station crew went on to tell me that the client had now been in a fight with another alpha psychopath over the cigarette trade and was currently in isolation. Ignore the diagnosis. It was the first time I had heard the term 'alpha' applied in such a situation, and I didn't know if it was legitimate. They were telling me that my prospective client was dangerous. Coming from them, staff dealing with clients on a day-to-day basis, one should never ignore it. The man's file supported their view by describing how he had killed his first two men at 13 years of age. I won't tell what they had done to him before he shot them. After mulling over the facts the ward supervisors had presented, and wondering how far the sense of humour of the director who had given me the assignment stretched—sometimes it isn't easy being the new kid on the block—I asked to be taken to see my prospective client. By this time, none of us were looking very enthusiastic about the task at hand.

A brief walk led to the first honest-to-God rubber room I had seen. It had the complete kit, including rubber walls and floor, no outlets, light switches unavailable, and recessed lights covered by mesh. My prospective client was standing in the center of the room naked, except for his jockey shorts. He was Caucasian, around six-foot-two, weighed somewhere around 220 pounds, and was very handsome. In fact, he seemed to be almost too handsome. I used my title while introducing myself and offering my hand. His grip felt flaccid. (I had occasionally experienced such grips in strong-looking men in various situations over the years. It always surprised me and gave me pause. Such behaviour might occur for any number of reasons.)

Considering that previous attempts to test my prospective client had failed, it was a surprise when he agreed to come with me to the testing room. At first, I thought he was just bored but then realized that the tin of mints I had in my shirt pocket could give the impression of being a tin of chewing tobacco. (The options: He wanted to get out of the room; he came along to get tobacco; he wanted someone to talk to. My bet would be on all three, and I was pretty sure I would win the trifecta.) We went down the hall together with my client wearing the blue kimono staff had given him, and a large security officer trailing behind us. Despite his size, the officer was quiet and unobtrusive, blending into the background very well. He would become very present in a few moments.

Arriving at the testing room, I opened the door and walked in, hearing it close softly behind me. The room was tiny. There was one table taking up most of it, and I had just walked in with my back to a 220-pound potential threat. As the enormity of what I had done began surfacing, I started reviewing in my head such tidbits of information as to why the 'threat' was in the institution, and why he had been placed in a rubber room. To make things even 'better', my large, handsome client was probably going to be disappointed when he found out I only had mints, not tobacco.

There was just enough time to allow the regret for my precipitate action to take hold when there was a soft knock at the door, and a voice asked, "Doctor can I talk to you for a minute?"

It was the quiet guard, who not only had exquisite timing but apparently hadn't gone for a coffee break.

"Why, yes, of course!" I replied in my most masculine and, hopefully professional, voice.

Was that a quaver? It was hard to tell if it was from relief, or because I had screwed up! Sliding belly-to-belly past my client, I opened the door and slipped out.

Bending down, the security guard placed his lips close to my ear and whispered, "You aren't going to do that again, are you?"

The knot, which had begun relaxing in my belly, told me how right he was. I felt grateful for the lesson he had provided.

After lithely sliding back into the room, I stood with my back to the door and asked my client to move to the other side of the table. He had remained impassive throughout the entire sequence of events. (He probably thought I had screwed up, too.) For a moment, he looked like someone watching a roach or something else small he could crunch under his boot. When I looked again, however, his gaze seemed as impassive as it had been all along. After he sat down on the other side of the table, I sat down while offering him a mint. It ran a distant second in the preference stakes, but he took it. He was bored and probably hoping for tobacco. He wanted to get out of that padded cell and talk to someone, too. He didn't do the testing but would do so during our next meeting. On this occasion, he did keep me talking long enough to finish my mints. I didn't mention the training workshop provided by the security guard in my report, though I did mention that my client and I had completed an interview. That quietly closing door had been a wake-up call for me. There would be others.

It was 8 p.m. when I entered the coffee room and saw an elderly doctor of forensic psychiatry. He was someone respected, even loved, by all. After over 45 years of service dealing with virtually every evil perpetrated by humans, he was still standing. I was looking at a long and admirable history central to my present interest and had just been lucky enough to get a chance to talk to him without others around. He was easy to approach, so asking questions would likely be welcomed.

After introducing myself, and telling him what I was doing in the institution we were working in, I asked him, "What do you believe to be the most dangerous condition in our clients?"

After a brief pause, he said, "I believe the most dangerous condition to be depression."

Mulling his response over and feeling encouraged by his friendliness as well as his thoughtful answer, I continued by asking him if he had ever been attacked over the years? He told me that he hadn't. By this time, he had gone to sit down and had waved me to a seat near him.

We drank coffee and discussed some of the clients I was seeing before I asked my third question in a comfortable silence: "How did you achieve such an admirable safety record while working in the forensic area for so many years, anyway? After the short time I have been working in the area, I felt the potential for being assaulted to be quite high."

It looked like he might have been thinking about the issue since he considered the question only briefly before replying. "I have tried to deal directly and honestly with the problems my clients were facing. I have also tried not to crowd anyone, and always left a person a way out."

His words stood me in good stead throughout the years. The idea of not crowding people proved to be particularly important during a situation that arose in a jail a few years later.

Guards, who were members of the institutional reaction team, had an inmate trapped in a room, and he was asking for someone to come in and talk to him. The team could take him down, but they were reluctant to do so if it wasn't necessary. They thought he wanted to come out, and probably would with some help. The senior correctional officer (SCO) approaching me wanted to know if I was willing to go in and talk to the man. He said the fellow was an oddball; flaky, and distressed. There was a lot of arguing in the trapped man's background, but the SCO didn't feel he was particularly violent. His main worry in the situation was that he wouldn't be able to see me after I went in. And it would take them some time to get to me if something went wrong. He ended by telling me I didn't have to do it. The 'out' he was giving, though kind and truthful, struck me as an invitation to be the topic of conversation for the next month. If push came to shove, it wasn't anything the guards there would be unwilling to do themselves, either. Besides, neither rain, nor snow, nor leaky bowels…

I had never passed in front of a reaction team before. They were pumped behind all those visors, shields, truncheons, and helmets! Moving through the door, I saw my date, who was also pumped, and vibrating like a harp! Closing the door slowly behind me, I stood there looking at him. Needless to say, I didn't do this every day and had little idea about what I should do, or say. Up to this point, I had been concentrating on getting to the room without any embarrassing side trips. Then I remembered that night in the coffee room, and what I had been told by that wonderful old forensic psychiatrist. So, how does one not crowd someone when in the situation my new client and I were currently in? I heard myself say, "How in the hell am I going to stay in this room with you, and not have you kick the living shit out of me?"

It was a proud moment! Thank you, old, and venerated teacher, wherever you are!

He answered, with his voice a-quaver in rhythm with his bodily vibrations: "If I come toward you, you move back, and I'll stop, OK?"

So, that is what we did. Eventually, after talking and dancing back and forth for a while, I told him I would turn my back, and he could put his hand on my shoulder, then we would walk out together. After we went out the door, he didn't resist when they took him down, and they didn't hurt him. The problem had been resolved peacefully thanks to good staff and advice from a fine old psychiatrist.

One day guards brought up another individual to see me for a visit. He was in manacles and looked very small between the two large guards beside him. All three of them had serious looks on their faces. They had also come from up from the isolation area—called the digger—which generally meant nothing good. After I politely asked the guards to take the manacles off, they hesitated briefly before doing so.

Then as they moved toward the door leaving me alone with my client, one of them said, "We'll be right outside!"

What was going on looked serious, but I still didn't have a clue what had happened. I felt my prospective client didn't have *the look*, though I could be fooled by that. It was to be an interesting session. I would recall what was said to me by that old psychiatrist, and I would use techniques developed by other psychologists. An added bonus was that I would also do some personal learning myself, though I wouldn't realize it until driving home that evening.

After regarding my client for a moment, I asked, "How come you are up here seeing me?"

Remembering the coffee room and the old psychiatrist, I was dealing with the problem directly.

Looking at me suspiciously, he said, "Fighting."

This was not necessarily the problem; being small and in jail, he'd better be willing to fight. It could be necessary. *It must have been one hell of a fight*, I thought. What happened? What is the problem?

"A guy called me a hound and I hit him."

That was the problem. Hound was a bad word. But he was dealing with words, not a physical assault. It was a flat statement, but mildly defensive, like he was saying that he could hit someone again. I didn't experience it as much of a threat. We might even be making progress. Then, with my brain in neutral, I said, "That's just great! He fucks up, and you do the hard time!"

This was directly dealing with the problem, but it was also an instinctive reaction and risky. As much as I would like to deny it, there was some luck involved here. It was where I was doing some figuring of my own and didn't know it. Looking at me, my client seemed to be trying to decide what kind of rock I had crawled out from under—better and better. He had good control and didn't look insulted. Everything was still hanging in the balance.

Getting up and heading for the door almost by reflex, I said, "Let's go out into the hall!"

He was looking very suspicious now! No one likes dealing with a crazy man, and the guards were out there, too. (It was another situation where I turned my back to someone. We were now up to three times. So, where are the differences between the situations?)

Since I had already walked over and opened the door, what could my client do, stay in the room? He followed me out. After looking at us, the guards moved a bit further away and I went in the other direction about 10 feet or so away from my client. He just stood there near the door looking like he was still wondering what was going on.

Looking at him, I said, "Call me a hound!"

I saw this as dealing directly with the problem. I could have used *Goof*, which was also a bad word at that time, but *hound* was more pointed.

"Fuck off!" he said.

Yup, willing to fight. Fuck off! was good, especially the tone he used. He was being reasonably friendly, while still trying to figure out what was going on. Being very careful about it, I kept begging and wheedling until he became convinced that I wouldn't stop asking.

So, he tried to make me stop. "OK," he said. "You're a hound!"

Now we were making progress. Getting the response I wanted, I did the bullfighting cape and let what he said fly by. Still looking for a smile, and maybe getting a small one, I asked him to call me a hound a couple of more times while I did the cape. He was catching on, and even beginning to enjoy it. So, I introduced the opening-a-hole-in-the-body routine. Intaking breath slowly for four seconds, I used my hands to signal opening a hole in my body. Then, holding my breath for four seconds, I let the word hound fly through while looking over my shoulder to watch it go away. Closing my hands after watching the hound disappear, I looked toward my client and slowly exhaled. Damned if he didn't catch onto that one, too.

We practiced, and he even let me call him names a couple of times. On one occasion, he didn't copy me but ducked instead. We were on our way to a good session. We talked about taking care of one's case, things a guy could say, and issues to deal with while doing the movements. We even considered the position of authority I was operating from, and what I could get away with that he might not. Even the toughest guys in jail are carrying a hundred-pound weight on their shoulders when dealing with those carrying some authority. They usually cut some slack for such people. They wouldn't for him.

He was starting to think about how not to trigger the aggression from the other person. Maybe, he would have some options when he went back or would look for some. He wasn't the fastest current in the brook, but he was fast enough. He needed to learn more about protecting himself without using violence.

It wasn't until driving home after the session that I tuned in to my own developmental needs. After making the turn onto the highway I began wondering how often someone else had fucked up, and I had done hard time? (There was my problem.) Some kind of switch closed, with that thought. I would still get my pocket picked by wrong words spoken from time to time. And I might end up doing hard time once in a while. But now I knew about one of the struggles I was in. Maybe that young man would be as lucky as I was finding that out!

ENDING

There was rising water and the intent gaze of a cougar when I was waking up during my earliest years. Many things were happening in my small world, and many happened after I left for other worlds. Like any other human, there were successes and failures over the years and significant events, as well as those not so significant. Then things seemed to take on a different appearance. My level of physical activity began to drop while I was carrying an appetite designed to support jobs with very high daily caloric output. (Human Factor estimates for some of the jobs I held during early years were extremely high, in the five or six thousand calories per day range.) Having always been physically active, I wasn't aware of the calories I was expending. And with my attention directed toward other things, I wasn't particularly aware when my pattern was changing. The situation reminds me of the "Silent Stalkers" I encountered when I was young. I became increasingly interested in the academic side of life and, slowly but surely, I was on a journey toward carrying 265 pounds on a 180-pound frame. It must sound unbelievable that I wasn't aware of what was happening, but it is true, nevertheless. The change snuck up on me like that rising water and the silent cougar. Only this stalker wouldn't go away as those two did.

I had never been truly sick, but four visits to surgery occurred in three months. Waking up after the first visit, I had the sickest feeling I had ever experienced in my life. It was all I could do to ask for something to help with nausea. The surgeon had even been forced to decide whether to cut a duct, a task that carried with it a 30%t chance of death. After my partner of many years, along with my mom—who lived to 93—left my room, I kept looking out the window at the traffic going up a large hill near the hospital. It was evening.

For many years, I had been aware of a transition in the lighting as evening approached. It became almost opalescent and reminded me of the revery state that precedes sleep. Going up the hill that evening,

169

the traffic I was watching became special. The cars seemed to slow down, and their headlights began to echo the evening light with their own muted opalescence. In that brief moment, I knew that the world would go on without me, much like the traffic was doing. In a way, it was such a simple thing, but for just an instant, a powerful feeling of loss and acceptance accompanied the travelling cars.

Of course, others have had such experiences, and some of theirs were even more monumental. I met a man who had been buried alive, for example. He described how his whole life changed radically after the experience. My life changed, too, though in less obvious ways than his. But the ending we all know is coming was present, and I felt it. Knowing where that feeling of loss began would take more time.

Retirement came, along with some withdrawal, as we moved to our small farm. There was beauty there and worthwhile physical work. Much of it came from returning to the country for me, especially cutting wood for the winter, working on our house, and doing fairly easy projects with wood and metal. There were new skills to develop, and my partner had introduced me to the world of art. She had helped confirm my belief, having read Robert Browning, that art precedes science, so I even built a small log cabin for an exhibit in the local museum. But someone burned down the museum, and the cabin was lost. Perhaps it was time for it to go, so I didn't rebuild it. My hunting for game gradually changed to target shooting of one kind or another as I removed myself from the grief of taking life for my food. I still accepted the importance of hunting as a moral act, but I had more than paid my dues and had done so respectfully.

Changes accompanied my emotional acceptance of death's approach. I began mourning the loss of the things around me, especially beautiful things. Looking at the big cottonwoods on our land, and listening to the wind hissing through them while making their leaves flash off and on with reflected light, would bring a sense of beauty and loss. Not having a heaven to go to, only an unconscious, silent darkness, that acute feeling of impending loss would continue to come over me when seeing beautiful things. It didn't happen all the time, but the bittersweetness of it struck once in a while. Nor did I spend hours categorizing all the things that would go. An appreciation of how some adverse events would also be losses appeared, but they would remain less critical—appreciation of their loss related to their resolution. The sense of regret from losing positive and negative experiences enriched my life. I began using the emotional acceptance of life's passing to remind me to pay attention and stay 'in' precious moments.

Accepting death strengthened the need to find meaning in my life. The idea was not new to me; I could remember joking about the meaning of life during adolescence. But now, being closer to the end, life review was more compelling, and reminiscence happened more often. The task of finding meaning was made more accessible by writing stories. Finding stories to write proved to be pretty easy. Those you have read here are only a sampling of them. But where did that feeling of loss and acceptance start? Eventually, I found that the beginning happened by chance in my early 20s. And the search provided the logical ending to the stories written here so many years later.

Walking along a dike alone while carrying my shotgun at a place called Boundary Bay, I was lost in thought. My father and I had hunted for ducks there many times. So, a vague feeling that a duck might fly by was present, but I was surprised to hear a goose calling. The tide was a long way out, and looking toward the ocean, all that could be seen was a tiny speck circling over the sand. The goose's flight looked strange to me. It kept going round and round without landing or flying away. The chance of approaching close enough to such a bird while walking over sandy flats was very low. But having immediately gone into hunting mode, I had to try. We had never been able to bring home a goose for dinner.

Slowly walking out on the flats while keeping my face hidden by looking down at the sand, I kept sneaking occasional glances at the flying bird. Tension began building as I got closer and closer. Finally, long after I thought it would leave, the goose began flying away while continuing to call. I stood watching until I could no longer see it, and its calling had faded away. Feeling puzzled, I kept walking toward where the bird had been circling and found a dead goose lying on the sand. With its wings tucked into its sides, it looked like it had simply folded up and fallen rather than struggled. There were goose tracks all around it. Seeing it lying there, its story came into my mind, full-blown.

Someone had shot at the geese while they were flying. Too high for a clean kill, the dead goose was hit with enough lead for it to fly some distance before dying. (Some hunters believed they could shoot a shotgun at long range, and only a special few could.) I saw it closing its wings when it finally fell because I had seen ducks that died quickly fall and land the same way. Believing that geese mated for life, I knew in my heart that the goose that had been flying around and around was her mate. (It could have just as easily been the female flying away, but my mind made it male.) The flying goose had stayed for so long because it was calling her to fly away with him and didn't want to leave her. All I could do with the feeling that pierced me was stand there crying. I let the tears go because there was no one else around.

Eventually, feeling it was a sacred place, I left the dead goose there to be carried away by the sea. I believe that was the first time I truly felt the profound sense of loss that could occur in life. By this time, I had seen people killed, but I had never cried about a death. And I had never felt anything as powerful as what I felt when looking at the dead goose. The poignant feeling would continue from that time on. It always happened when I heard a flock of geese calling as they flew over, and it still does. The feeling is strongest when I listen to geese migrating on their long journey south. It was that time of year when I had left her on the sand to be carried away by the ocean.

Somehow, the sense of loss I felt when seeing the dead goose didn't connect to my own end as a human being at that time. That attachment began later. The ending I eventually chose came from Emily Carr, that strange, talented artist who admired First Nations people, understood nature, and could paint so well:

> Today at seventy I marvelled more at the migration of
> the geese than I had at the age of seven when standing in
> our cow pasture holding my father's hand and looking up
> into the sky, I heard Father tell the story of bird migration
> and only half-believed. What of the old or maimed goose
> who could not rise and go with the flock? Of course, there
> 'was' the old, maimed goose. What of him when the flock,
> young and vigorous, rose leaving him grounded? Did
> despair tear his heart? No old goose would fill the bitter

moment, pouring out proud, exultant honks that would weave among the clatter of the migrating flock. When the flock was away, animal-wise he would nibble here and nibble there, quietly accepting.

Old age has me grounded too. Am I accepting? God give me the brave unquestioning trust of the wild goose! No, being humans, we need more trust, our hopes are stronger than creatures' hopes.[14]

– Emily Carr (December 13, 1871 - March 2, 1945)

---

[14] *Growing Pains: The Autobiography of Emily Carr*, with a foreword by Ira Dilworth. Toronto: Oxford University Press, 1946.